MW01128166

"Lauryl Zenobi's *I want a U[...]* figuring out how to make th[...] other profession. The book [...] plates and samples that make the "how" absolutely clear, and pointers to numerous other resources. Lauryl serves as your friendly and enthusiastic coach through the process, sharing her own story and bringing to light the stories of a number of other researchers. As a bonus, the book also serves as a detailed ethnography of the work of user research, analyzing and describing the language, and practices, and shared cultural beliefs of the profession. I'm eager to recommend this book in all my future conversations with people making this professional change."

Steve Portigal,
Portigal Consulting (portigal.com)

"This book is packed full of actionable, practical advice for folks looking for their first job in UX Research. Lots of detailed information from somebody who's clearly done her research."

Laura Klein, Principal, Users Know
Author, *Build Better Products* and *UX for Lean Startups*

"In "I Want a UX Job" Lauryl presents important considerations for making the shift into the UX research world, including understanding the fundamentals about the field, what your typical work day looks like, how to find your UX community, crafting your resume so you speak the language of the hiring committee, getting that crucial experience in the field, and finally landing your first job.

Lauryl's pragmatic approach gives you a handbook with practical guidance, worksheets, and stories from UX practitioners who've been there, done that and succeeded to help you improve your chances at getting your foot in the door of your first UX research job. A must read for all UX Research fledglings!"

Rebecca Destello,
Research Manager, Facebook

"I want a UX job!" is a much needed book to help people just breaking into the field of User Experience Design. No matter where you're starting from, this book has practical, accessible advice and diverse stories about everything from training to resumes to interviewing. Much like the field itself, the book is full of empathy and understanding for the reader who may be at a crossroads in their life and is in need of mentorship. I highly recommend this book for anyone looking to get a job in the UX field!

Julie Kientz, Professor & Chair,
Human Centered Design & Engineering,
University of Washington

"Succinct, systematic, eminently practical, and thoughtful approach to navigating your transition to UX.

All too often, advice on transitioning into the UX field makes it sound like happenstance or luck: "I was already doing design then I got curious about the research side" or "I was in the right places at the right time" There are magical unicorns that get swept up in a UX wave and never look back. For everyone else, there's Lauryl Zenobi.

I spent an immense amount of time in my life in my late 20 and early 30s reflecting, researching, reading, and stressing about what I wanted to do with my life. Lauryl talks about transitioning to a new career being so difficult because our identities are bound up in our work. The book is peppered with real stories that take this step by step workbook out of the aspirational and into the practical realm. As much as it is a thoughtful step by step, how-to (buy it for the interview guide alone folks) it is also a hope bringer. It puts you in charge of an overwhelming process. Without giving away the key elements, the steps guide you in a way that seem eminently doable. In a world full of books suggesting 200 page annotated bullet journals and excel sheets with pivot tables, Zenobi's streamlined methods are a breath of fresh air."

Dr. Nichole Carelock,
Special Projects Director at Tech Talent Project

"Lauryl has written a wonderful guide on how to change careers into the rewarding and growing field of user experience research. Her book lays out what skill sets you'll need to develop and how to do it.

Based on my own career change — from technical theater to UX research — I think her most valuable advice here is how to market yourself as a researcher. She shows how to demonstrate your existing research skills by describing your previous work through a UX lens and by using the language of this industry. You're not starting from scratch. You already have more experience than you might think!

Changing careers can be scary. Lauryl shows you where to begin and has included many stories from people who have done it successfully. I wish I'd had this roadmap when I was planning to enter the field."

Angela Colter,
Former Executive Director of 18F

I WANT A
UX
JOB!

HOW TO MAKE A CAREER
CHANGE INTO UX RESEARCH

LAURYL ZENOBI

Illustrations by Brian A. Prince, www.thebaprince.com

Cover and Interior Design by Steve Kuhn, www.kuhndesigngroup.com

ISBN #9798696988184

© 2020 Lauryl Zenobi

www.laurylzenobi.com
www.iwantauxjob.com

CONTENTS

INTRODUCTION

first started writing about UX research in 2015. Since then, rarely a week goes by without someone reaching out to me seeking advice on making their own transition into UX research. UX researchers, also known as user experience (UX) researchers or user researchers, are the folks that speak with users before a product is built, and who test a product during and after it is built to make sure that it meets the needs of the people who will ultimately use the product.

After the first dozen or so emails and DMs and video calls, I realized there was a real hunger for more information on how to make this career leap. This made me curious enough to ask colleagues and peers how they got into UX research—and as I started asking around, I came to realize that my story was not that unique.

In fact, my story was incredibly similar to that of my colleague, Nichole Carelock.

Nichole fell into UX research accidentally as well. Her UX origin story begins when she was living in Houston, Texas. At the time, she worked with a Community Technology Center (CTC) to bring computer labs and technology to under-served areas. When Hurricane Katrina hit, refugees from New Orleans and elsewhere in Louisiana started pouring into Houston, and the Center got involved in relief efforts. When Nichole showed up to the Astrodome with blankets, food, and other relief supplies, the scale of the disaster was almost incomprehensible. When she talks about that time, she says, "They housed thousands of people inside of the Astrodome." Poor African American communities were overrepresented in the refugee camps.

As Nichole started talking to hurricane victims, she kept hearing the same refrain: "Thank you for the blankets, but actually I don't know where my grandmother is?" "Can you help me find my people?" After many conversations like this, she realized there was a better solution.

According to Nichole, "The rescue effort was so disparate. People were in Seattle. People were in Houston. People were in Minnesota." What Nichole heard in these tense conversations were the real needs of these refugees. This prompted her to work with Yahoo to build a database so hurricane refugees could locate their family members. The CTC set up computers in the middle of the Astrodome for people to search this database for their loved ones, or add their own location so that others could search for them.

Nichole remembers how it felt when people started using the database: "People would go down to the floor of the Astrodome and try to find their grannies, find their uncles. When they found a person, they would have a huge cowbell to ring. That moment of ringing the cowbell was just *such a moment.*

It's the difference between what you think needs to happen, what seems obvious—blankets, food, and talking to someone—and realizing what is actually a better solution."

Because of her experience with Katrina relief efforts, Nichole decided to get a doctorate in anthropology, focusing on how people use technology. But while working in a post-doc position in Philadelphia, she started to experience the realities of finding a tenure-track position in the crowded and competitive world of academia. A steady trickle of no after no followed every academic application she put out. Meanwhile, the university's business school kept knocking on the anthropology department's door to see if any of the anthropologists there were interested in helping them run UX research studies. Nichole started to recognize that there was an industry need for the human-focused skills she had mastered during her doctoral studies. Not only was there a desire for research in technology and business, but there was value attached to her research skills. Nichole reflects, "It was like, 'We value what you do so much that we are going to pay you for this two-hour intervention.' Oh, well, sir, you had me at value."

Nichole started with small consulting gigs, gradually building up a skill set and branching out into larger projects. The need and desire for research skills in a business or technology setting became obvious.

But Nichole feared her application seemed too academic, so she started to market her skills in a new way. She says, "I made the mistake for a long time of saying, I'm an anthropologist who can do this research. It was very hard for me to detach myself from the work that I'd done for seven and eight years. My LinkedIn, my resumes, they all said, 'She's an academic.'"

Like Nichole, I came to UX research from an academic background in anthropology and archaeology. Most UX professionals enter the field from tangentially related careers, making either an intentional or accidental shift into UX research. Many of us found ourselves in these careers without much guidance, driven by necessity to figure things out as we went.

The longer I've been a researcher, the more stories I've heard like my own and like Nichole's. There's a knowledge gap between those who are in UX careers and those who are trying to break into the field. How do you get into UX research? How do you approach a career transition to UX? How do you reconfigure your identity as an academic, as a recent college graduate, as someone changing careers mid-life? How do you reinvent yourself? These are questions that this book will help you answer.

> One of the most unexpectedly daunting parts of transitioning to UX research was coming to terms with my new professional identity. I had spent six years identifying as an architectural designer and researcher.
>
> PREETI TALWAI, UX RESEARCHER AT GOOGLE AI*

WHAT IS UX RESEARCH?

At its core, UX research is about spending time with the "users" of a product, learning about their needs and taking those insights to improve the product. That product might be laundry soap, an iPhone app, a car, or a website—UX researchers work in all these industries and more. While the term "user experience research" is certainly more common these days, it's not a well-understood job to most folks outside of tech companies. Like many researchers, when asked what I do, I'll respond with something along the lines of this: "I talk with people about how they use websites so that we can make them better and easier to use."

It's not just the general public that struggles to understand what UX research means—even those who may have heard of UX research aren't entirely sure how to move into the field. Until very recently, UX as a field wasn't an official major in college, and programs teaching human-centered design (HCD), UX design, and UX research are still relatively

* Preeti Talwai "Finding a voice as a non-traditional UX researcher" www.medium.com/
google-design/finding-a-voice-as-a-non-traditional-ux-researcher-d58e66c3f80b

rare. It's increasingly common to get post-educational training through bootcamps or micro-degree programs, which provide a crash course on research and design fundamentals to those preparing for a career change into UX. The majority of new UX professionals, however, have to learn how to leverage their non-UX experiences and training to get hired into their chosen research or design role. The process of moving into UX isn't particularly challenging or inaccessible; rather, the problem is that there is no single resource that defines what that process looks like. Every single person who reaches out to me asks, "You did this, now how do I do this?"

The more conversations I had with folks wanting to transition to UX research, the more I saw a need to talk about my experiences with the process. There are dozens and dozens of books on how to do research, but there aren't many resources outside of blog posts and the occasional conference talk on how to get into research. My hope is this book will be that resource for you.

If you are reading this book, you are likely in a state of in-between, moving from one space to another. For many people, these transitory periods in life can be difficult to navigate emotionally. This is because moving from one space to another by nature requires you to change your identity and how you perceive yourself, even in a minor way.

For some of you, this transitional space might be that you just graduated from college and are looking for your first job. Perhaps you are finishing up your graduate work and aren't sure how your prospects on the academic market will pan out. Or you might have picked up this book because you are in the depths of a career you no longer find satisfying, and you're interested in exploring a new field. Whoever you are, I ask that you read this book with an open mind, take what works for you, throw out what doesn't, and be gentle with yourself. Moving into UX research requires a lot of learning, bravery, and a sense of adventure!

Each chapter of this book will give you tools and ideas to guide your transition into UX research. Along the way, I've included interviews from UX researchers who have come from all walks of life and have agreed to share their stories in this book. UX research is a storytelling profession, and it would be equivalent to malpractice if I didn't include others' voices. Hopefully, some of my interviewees' stories will resonate with you.

While the book is meant to be read sequentially, each chapter can stand alone, so if you need to read up on building a portfolio but aren't yet interested in how to interview or look for a job, you can easily bounce back and forth between chapters. You will, however, gain the most by reading the book cover to cover, since it's organized to map out your journey into UX research.

My hope is that this book will allow you to take a step back and enjoy this roller coaster of a process while giving you concrete steps and insights that allow you to make measurable progress towards your goal of moving into a career in UX research.

WHAT DOES THIS PROCESS LOOK LIKE?

This book is set up to mirror the process that I, and many other researchers, have taken. Each chapter focuses on a critical stage of the process, building on the previous material as you progress through the book. At the end of each chapter is a "What to read now" section that gives you additional resources that go deeper into the subjects covered in that chapter. While those additional resources aren't required readings, they add a lot of context and give you exposure to other researchers.

The links to "What to read now" chapter resources and any other websites I cite are organized by chapter at

www.iwantauxjob.com

STEP
0

LEARN THE FUNDAMENTALS

Before you even start to apply for jobs, you'll need to build out your foundation as a researcher. Start here with the Monster List of UX Books*, which is built and maintained by Chris Oliver. I discovered Chris's list recently and it's incredibly useful for researchers of any level of experience. I have also put together a list of must-read books that are fundamental for UX researchers, all of which are resources I still refer to myself. Start on these books right away! You can easily find them on Amazon or at large bookstores.

Steve Krug *Don't Make Me Think*

Steven Portigal *Interviewing Users*

Laura Klein *UX for Lean Startups: Faster, Smarter User Experience Research and Design*

---

* Monster List of UX Books
www.airtable.com/universe/expqM3OWZoJkjl7wy/the-monster-list-of-ux-books

Don Norman *Design of Everyday Things*

Erika Hall *Just Enough Research*

Leah Buley *The User Experience Team of One: A Research and Design Survival Guide*

William Albert and Thomas Tullis *Measuring the User Experience: Collecting, Analyzing, and Presenting Usability Metrics*

Braden Kowitz, et.al. *Sprint: How to Solve Big Problems and Test New Ideas in Just Five Days*

Dana Chisnell and Jeffrey Rubin *Handbook of Usability Testing: How to Plan, Design and Conduct Effective Test*

Chapter 1. Learn about the field

Learn what makes a good researcher, how to identify your transferable skills, and what to expect in terms of compensation and experience.

Chapter 2. Learn about the work

A crash course on the work-life of a researcher along with some perspective on the job market and hiring process. You'll start building out your transferable skills into an Experience List.

Chapter 3. Finding your community

Growing your UX network is a critical step in this process, and you'll identify resources that will help you develop a strong community.

Chapter 4. How to craft your resume

Enhance your Experience List from Chapter 2 and build out your UX resume and portfolio.

Chapter 5. How to get experience

Get experience to add to your resume and portfolio, and how to record it in ways that translate well to a hiring committee.

Chapter 6. How to find jobs

To land a job, you need to know where to look for one. Discover resources and develop strategies for finding or creating your first UX role.

Chapter 7. Interviewing

Interviewing is the final test in your process of moving into user research. Learn how to prepare for UX researcher interviews and what questions to expect.

Remember, this process will look a little different for everyone, so don't get caught up in following the steps to a T. This process will take time, so don't try to rush through all the resources included in this book over a single weekend. The more thoughtful you can be about the process, the more the information will sink in. Enjoy the ride!

LEARN ABOUT
THE FIELD

My first job out of grad school was at the American Anthropological Association, a non-profit academic association for anthropologists. I felt fortunate to have found a job in my field when so many of my recently graduated colleagues were still struggling to secure a postdoc or tenure-track position. Sure, it didn't pay a lot, but I was content to just have a paycheck after six months of unemployment!

Just before I got my non-profit job, my partner and I had moved to DC so he could take a job at 18F, a US government digital service agency that brings UX researchers, designers, and technologists together to work on complex projects for the federal government.

So here I was, a fresh master's degree in hand, fascinated with the real-world challenges my partner was trying to solve. It dawned on me that

I wasn't satisfied with the work that I was doing in my day job. I realized my skills and interests could help solve those real-world challenges, and this would satiate my desire for a career with a big impact.

I initially went into anthropology because I care about the state of the world and the curious, amazing things that people do. Anthropology programs teach you to look at a topic holistically—always looking for the root cause of an issue—and develop culturally appropriate ways to resolve it. Anthropology looks at both the individual and the society at large. It trains you to ask questions and to use the answers to those questions to create solutions.

Anthropology is an incredibly rewarding degree. But let's be honest, there aren't many anthropology jobs. That realization, along with my previously mentioned desire for a career with an impact, is what started me down the UX research path. This path eventually led me to my current position as a Senior UX Researcher, where I get to mentor and grow other researchers and work on challenging projects.

But when I started where you are right now, this book didn't exist yet. I spent eighteen months muddling my way through the transition into UX research, and I learned a lot about what did and didn't work. I wasted lots of time on things that weren't useful, but occasionally got lucky and stumbled onto a few things that were.

The process outlined in the introduction is what I wish someone gave me when I first started thinking about a career change. I did most of these steps out of order. I over-designed and over-thought resume after resume, used a buck-shot approach to apply for jobs that were bad fits at companies I had no interest working for, and I had no idea how to advocate for myself or my experiences. I was anxious throughout the process because I didn't know if I was doing this career change right. And for good reason—there was no guide for what I was doing!

There's a real mental shift that needs to occur when you move into a new field or career, and UX research is no different. You need to learn new research skills and become familiar with the expectations of research jobs.

WHAT DOES IT TAKE TO BE A UX RESEARCHER?

Perhaps you're already convinced that you want to be a UX researcher. Perhaps you've picked up this book because you're not quite sure what it means to be a UX researcher and you're interested in learning more. Or perhaps you've been gifted this book by a friend or loved one who wants you to finally settle on a career (rude). Regardless of how you happened upon this book, welcome! Let's dive into what it takes to be a UX researcher.

UX research, like many careers rooted in the social sciences, requires an interesting mix of "hard" and "soft" skills. Before I go too deep, let's take a moment and talk about what "hard" and "soft" skills even mean.

Hard skills are the "what" of UX research. These are the methodological, analytical, and precise skills that research needs to justify a level of rigor. Running a robust survey, establishing a rigorous research methodology, or generating statistical analysis are all examples of hard skills when it comes to UX research.

Hard skills you need as a researcher

- **Survey methodology**, including understanding the structure and pacing of a survey to minimize the likelihood of scoring biases or errors based on poorly formulated question/answer styles.

- **Statistical analysis**, especially when dealing with large

data sets such as those produced by surveys, Google analytics, or other website/app performance analytics.

- **Domain-specific knowledge**, such as how APIs work,
  how a medical device functions, or how a database is built
  or managed. You'll pick this knowledge up in your new
  role, so if you're not expert in this stuff yet, don't worry!

Soft skills are the "how" of UX research. The hard skills are meaningless without the soft skills, since you need soft skills to execute the hard
skills. Soft skills are the interpersonal skills, such as intuiting when to
dive deeper into a line of questioning with a user, or how your personality comes across during interviews. Soft skills for UX research are
traits that are traditionally viewed in Western culture as feminine. In
fact, the majority of UX researchers are women (or identify as women).
Most cultures train women in these soft skills as a natural part of growing up (interestingly, one of the few cases where sexism gives us a leg
up in the workforce).

All that, unsurprisingly, means that UX research is one area of tech, at
least in the US, where women outnumber men. That is slowly changing as more and more people realize that a range of life experiences and
gender identities are needed to understand the diversity of users and
build better products. If you're a man (or male-identifying person) reading this, please don't think a career in UX research is not a good fit for
you. UX research is truly accessible to anyone who is interested in devel-
oping their empathy and listening skills, regardless of gender identity.

Soft skills you need as a researcher

- **Empathy.** This is the ability to approximate what a user
  feels and the world they operate in.

- **Curiosity.** A researcher is interested in uncovering the why.

- **Sense of humility and an awareness of your own biases.** This is the recognition that who you are as a person and your experiences will always color your observations as a researcher. Functionally, you need to understand how to separate yourself (e.g., your opinions, what you would do) from what your users do.

- **Well-guided intuition.** A researcher must know when to dive in deeper with a user, or when to move on to a new topic of research.

- **Conscientiousness and responsibility.** A researcher needs to be good at both small details like correctly labeling studies or scheduling a participant, as well as larger-scale responsibilities such as managing confidentiality and curating research findings.

- **Collaboration and independence.** A researcher will need to work with a variety of personalities and disciplines, but they might also be the sole researcher on a team and need to carry the weight of research responsibilities on their own.

One reason that UX research is an easy transition from many different backgrounds and disciplines is because of the nature of these soft skills. Most of these skills are not learned through a degree, but rather through a variety of life experiences and interests. Any reasonably motivated person can learn basic statistics or research methodologies, but it takes a well-developed set of soft skills to be able to put someone at ease during a usability test, or be able to convince a reluctant stakeholder with a well-crafted presentation that promotes user empathy.

When I'm hiring researchers, I look for five things to assess these hard and soft skills:

1. Rigorous training in methodology

2. Experience with project management

3. High degree of professionalism

4. Ability to collaborate

5. Writing and presentation skills

Let's break down each one in detail.

A rigorous training in methodology

Experience in methodology means you'll be able to advocate for the right method, ask the right questions, justify your choices, and get your stakeholders on the right path. UX researchers will be familiar with a few core methods like usability testing, moderated interviews, and survey design, and broadly familiar with other methods like tree-testing or focus group moderation. The books listed in Step 0 in the introduction will help you build out your expertise.

Experience with project management

UX researchers need a deep understanding of what project management takes—without it, you won't be able to advocate for when and how research is done. In many cases, UX researchers are the only people in a company or on a team who are familiar with human-focused research methods, so you'll be responsible for doing right by your research goals and your users. This includes maintaining a high level of research ethics. Past experiences with project management will look like managing timelines, budgets, hiring or supervising employees, or figuring out project scope and success metrics. If you have these types of experiences, make sure to talk about them on your resume and in your interviews!

A high degree of professionalism

UX researchers are often the face of a company and interact directly with its users. You can have a big impact on how much users trust your company's product based on their interactions with you. In a company where research isn't a high priority, the way you conduct yourself will impact how seriously you and your results are taken. Being professional both in research sessions and with your colleagues will help you increase your users' trust in the company and build bridges between teams at work.

The ability to collaborate

As a UX researcher, you will need to work with a variety of stakeholders, product managers, development teams, designers, and marketing teams. Companies care a lot about your ability to collaborate and be a team player. Remember, research is a social endeavor—rarely do you work in silos. You will need to rely on a network of other researchers and colleagues to collect, curate, analyze, and share data (see Chapter 5).

Writing and presentation skills

The greatest skill a researcher has is the ability to translate a user's needs into a compelling story and present it to decision-makers. Researchers are conduits between companies and their customers, so it's ultimately up to you to present users' needs in a way that allows your company to take action and make choices about the product's design and functions. How well you write and talk about your research results will directly affect how seriously your research is taken.

WHO ARE RESEARCHERS?

In terms of backgrounds, researchers are quite diverse. Historically we've come from a wide number of fields, because until recently, UX research was not offered as an undergraduate degree, graduate degree, or professional certificate. As the field matures, however, it's become more common to see folks enter UX research from programs that focus on UX research and human-centered design.

Regardless, the field is incredibly varied in experience and expertise. Once in UX, many people specialize in certain settings and domains: digital versus analog products, start-ups and early-stage companies versus established companies, small teams versus large teams, government or non-profit versus private-sector companies.

Something a lot of UX researchers have in common is a graduate degree. Most of the people who reach out to me for advice on transitioning into UX research are finishing up a master's or PhD. This makes sense, as many of the skills that you learn in graduate programs translate very well to the world of UX research.

A graduate degree can give you a leg up when you apply for a UX research position, especially at large tech companies, but it is not necessary. Advanced training prepares you for both the hard and soft skills that are needed in a UX career, but it certainly isn't the only way to get a UX job. Anyone with a curiosity drive and an ability to listen deeply will make an excellent researcher. Sure, graduate degrees train students in those skills, but you don't need a university to teach you how to listen.

You may decide after reading this book that you do want to pursue a degree in UX research. Great! Over the course of these chapters, you may also decide that you absolutely do not want to go back to school. Also great! There is no tried-and-true path to UX research. This book is a synthesis of what worked for myself and others, and I expect that some of the advice here will challenge you and push you out of your comfort zone. Ultimately, it is your path to create based on your circumstances, timeline, and career goals.

SETTING EXPECTATIONS

Now that you have a sense of who researchers are and what skills they use, it's time to learn about the job market that UX researchers work in. The best way to reduce fear about something is to know that thing inside and out.

When it comes to compensation, you can do some research on typical salaries for that position at that company through tools like Glassdoor and UXPA salary studies. According to industry surveys*, the average entry-level salary in the US in 2019 was about $85,000. Compensation levels will obviously vary depending on the city you reside in and the local job market. Tech giants (Google, Microsoft, Amazon, Facebook) pay on the higher end of the scale, whereas a new start-up will pay on the lower end. Internship roles at a large company like Amazon will be paid, but might not be at a small company. While most positions, especially those in tech-focused cities and hot job markets, require graduate-level training, entry-level positions are open to those at the bachelor's level.

Dive into what each company expects in terms of years of experience. A mid-level research role at a small company might be more forgiving in terms of experience than a similar job at Facebook. An entry-level role in a big tech city might ask for more experience than an entry-level role in a city with a smaller tech scene. Take time to build up your knowledge on your local or desired job market. This will help you set your expectations, point out where you can grow to make yourself a more attractive candidate, and allow you to focus on roles and companies that will be a good fit for you. All of this will make the job search much smoother.

Remember: the number of UX research jobs is continuing to grow, so there's no scarcity of roles. There's plenty of room for new researchers, and the field is continuing to grow and specialize. In certain markets, you will find research positions focused on healthcare, social media,

---

* Nielson Norman Group, Salary Trends for UX Professionals
  www.nngroup.com/articles/salary-trends-usability-professionals/

state or federal digital services, real estate, and more. There are so many areas where answers to "how can we make this work better for our users" is valued, and research skills play a critical role in a product's development or the functioning of a company.

Why is UX research growing? A large part of the growth is because of the value that research brings to a company's product. Imagine if Uber had never tested how to make people feel comfortable getting into a stranger's car that they summoned over an app? Or if Facebook had never tested reaction emojis instead of just a thumbs-up? Now think about how much these companies are worth on the stock market. Not incorporating research in any form (i.e., not validating that your product is something people want or not validating that it works the way users want it to) can cost a company untold sums of money and doom a product. When enough successful companies and tech leaders demonstrate the value that testing, iteration, and UX research bring to a product's success, it makes sense that the market catches on.

WHAT TO READ NOW

iwantauxjob.com/chapter1

Remember, all the chapter
resources are linked at this website!

Nadine Levin, "10 Things You Should Know about Moving from Academia to Industry"

Emma McCabe, "The (Non-Traditional) Way to Break Into UX Research"

Tatiana Vlahovic, "Becoming a UX researcher: my experience and things I've learned along the way"

Preeti Talwai, "Finding a Voice as a Non-Traditional UX Researcher"

Rachel Fleming, "So You're Interested in User Experience (UX) Research? Thoughts from an Anthropologist Working in Industry"

UXPA International, "2018 UX Salary Survey"

ZSOMBOR'S UX STORY

Zsombor Varnagy-Toth

Zsombor is a Senior UX Researcher and Research Lead for a B2B SaaS (Business-to-Business Software-as-a-Service) company, where he runs a team of seven researchers. Like many researchers I spoke with, Zsombor made the transition to UX research while finishing up his PhD. Zsombor is a great example of how to translate your previous experience and skills into the field of UX research. His experience offers perspectives on the job market and the skills needed to get hired.

Tell me about how you got started as a researcher. What has been your career path?

I had been an Assistant Research Fellow working on my PhD in cognitive science. I knew some IT stuff, wrote my own scripts, analyzed loads of data, worked with gaze-tracking. In the lab where I worked, we did some testing of various apps for kids with autism. Some of those were sort of usability tests, although much more elaborated methodologically. I had this growing feeling that this PhD and the resulting academic career was leading nowhere. That was when my daughter was born, and I realized I needed to make real money. So I literally typed in my skills into Google "cognitive psychology research job" and found a job posting at a company that contained all the search terms.

That was the first time I have ever heard about UX research. Then I researched it, applied for that job, got rejected, but by then I got the taste. So I went further, went to meetups, hooked up with a small design agency that was just starting out. I became their first researcher and did usability testing. I grew together with the agency, doing more and more kinds of UX research as we went.

When this UX job was consistently paying more (way more) than my academic job, I just quit academia and never looked back.

What do you think your previous jobs/educational experiences gave you as a researcher?

Basically, I knew all the methods and their background, cognitive psychology, and experimental psychology. I just didn't know how to apply those in the context of product development and had very little idea of product development itself.

Psychology gave me an approach to treat people with genuine curiosity, humility, and a non-judgmental attitude. These are extremely useful skills when doing qualitative research.

It also helped that a couple of us tried to launch our very own startup at the time I was transitioning into UX. That was when I first saw a business model canvas, and when I learned that a great experience is meaningless if the product doesn't solve an important enough problem. Because I was the consumer of the research, and not only the producer, I got to experience what kind of product decisions should those research activities support. Using my own research was eye-opening.

How would you talk about the job market for UX research?

Back then as a newbie, I had no problem with it. The market had opportunities for me even in such a small country like Hungary. Now that I have been on the hiring side for a while, I see that there is a stark disconnect between the demand and the supply side of UX researchers. On the one hand, there are a lot of great companies looking for researchers. But they are all looking for already experienced researchers who can hit the ground running. This is due to the fact that they are looking to hire their first researcher or their team is small, so they have no time to teach someone new. On the supply side, we have only a handful of experienced researchers and an abundance of noobs who are not ready to do a research role independently. Even in our company, our design team has eighteen people, one of the biggest in the country, and even we aren't able to raise our own researchers. There is so much work to do; many of us work on multiple product teams at the same time.

What are some stumbling blocks that people getting into research might experience? What barriers do you see in the field?

Getting hands-on skills seems to be the biggest obstacle. In 2014, Jacob Nielsen wrote that 10% of this craft is learned in classrooms but a good 90% of it comes through on-the-job learning. As someone who hires researchers, I can confirm that. Novices come out of school, they have heard about all the practices they need to do, but when they actually do the job, they get disorientated very quickly. UX research is a craft where you need to do ten different things simultaneously. You can only do this if nine out of those ten are already in your procedural memory (that is, you can do it without thinking about it).

Actually, I just started a little project initiative to bridge this gap: uxmicromasteries.com. There is this catch-22 situation where you learn these skills on the job, but you don't get the job without the skills. There are ways to learn these skills outside the job as well. You just need to know what these mysterious, unspoken skills are and how to approach them.

LEARN ABOUT
THE WORK

What do I do all day? What does a typical week look like? How long are my projects? Whenever I do informational interviews, these are the most common questions from people interested in getting into UX research. And they are great questions! You definitely want to know what your day-to-day work will look like before you make a big career move.

My work cadence is rarely typical. I might have a full day of meetings with stakeholders one day, and half a day of company meetings another day. One week might be full of user sessions, the next full of analysis work. Each industry and company will have a slightly different cadence for research work. In government work, a project might last two or more years. In a consulting company, you might engage with a client for only two weeks.

Here are a few examples of my daily schedules:

EXAMPLE MEETING DAY	
9:30AM	DAILY TEAM MEETING ("STAND-UP")
10:00AM	KICK OFF FOR NEW PROJECT WITH CLIENT
11:00AM	ONE-ON-ONE MEETING WITH TEAM MEMBER
12:00PM	LUNCH/TAKE DOG TO PARK
1:00 - 2:00PM	RESEARCH TEAM SYNC
2:00PM	COMPANY ALL HANDS MEETING (DOG WOULD LIKE TO GO TO THE PARK AGAIN PLEASE)
3:00 - 5:00PM	ADMIN WORK

You'll notice a lot of strange meeting names that are common in tech companies. Many of these terms borrow from design and development methods like Agile, Lean, and Scrum. I recommend having a passing familiarity with these methods, because they serve as a lingua franca between product, development, design, and research teams. (These methods are covered in the "Must-Read Books" section of the Introduction, but a quick online search will also give you a good understanding of the core goals and values for each.)

EXAMPLE RESEARCH DAY	
7:30AM	TAKE DOG TO DAYCARE (ENJOYS PEACE AND QUIET)
8:00 - 8:45AM	USABILITY SESSION PARTICIPANT #1
9:00 - 9:45AM	USABILITY SESSION PARTICIPANT #2
10:00 - 10:45AM	USABILITY SESSION PARTICIPANT #3
1:00 - 1:45PM	USABILITY SESSION PARTICIPANT #4
2:00 - 2:45PM	USABILITY SESSION PARTICIPANT #5
3:00 - 3:45PM	USABILITY SESSION PARTICIPANT #6

During a stand-up meeting, all members of the team will talk about what they're working on, where they are making progress, where they might be stuck, and what they would like help on.

Kick-off meetings are for setting project expectations and getting an introduction to what the client would like to see from the project.

One-on-one meetings are where I'll connect with a fellow team member, provide mentorship, talk about their thoughts on the project, or set up quarterly goals.

Team syncs are where all the researchers (and sometimes all the designers) in the company get together and talk about various projects or company-wide research initiatives.

All-hands are company-wide meetings where the CEO will give a weekly update on how the company is doing and what is coming down the pipeline.

My admin work tends to look like prepping reviews, setting goals, filling out my timesheet, etc.

EXAMPLE ANALYSIS DAY	
9:30AM	DAILY TEAM MEETING ("STAND-UP")
10:00AM - 3:00PM	WRITE TRANSCRIPTS
3:30PM	RESEARCH TEAM CHECK-IN
4:00 - 5:00PM	CODING
5:30PM	TAKE DOG TO DOG PARK

As you can see from my example work schedules, my dog requires a lot of exercise, and I might only spend one day a week with users. The rest of the time is client meetings, team meetings, and admin work.

During a typical month, only about 20% of my time is spent in user sessions. This percentage will vary depending on the industry and company. For example, a researcher at a consultancy might spend most of their workday researching and analyzing to maximize billable hours and produce work quickly for a client. I have some leadership responsibilities in my current role, so I spend more of my time on mentorship, client-facing work, and admin tasks. Each role and company will have different expectations on how much time you spend on these different responsibilities.

It's the unfortunate reality that the best part of any job is often the part you do the least. For a UX researcher, that means you are not going to spend as much time as you'd like conducting research with end users. But don't despair! Just because you aren't researching with users doesn't mean you aren't researching. You'll use the same methods and skills from your work with users on your clients, stakeholders, and partner teams. Each group is their own type of user—they will use the research you produce in different ways, so treat your interactions with these groups as their own type of research session. Kick-off meetings, sync ups with development or product teams, and client meetings are all good opportunities to figure out what those users need from your research.

What do your marketing or sales teams need to sell the product? What does your development team need from you so they can write their code in a way that meets your customers' needs? What presentation styles work best with your client? You need to know all of these things so that you can tailor the user experience of your research output. It's a little meta, but it's important to remember that you have lots of user types, not just your end users or customers.

Now that you have a sense of the daily life of a researcher, let's talk about the long-term. You have a lot of options when it comes to career trajectory in UX research, and I have yet to see someone walk away from UX research because there is no new challenging role or next step in their career growth. There are so many industries to work in and interesting problems to solve, especially as technologies advance and companies care more about the UX of their products. If the endless slew of cool new products or specialties gets old for you, you can work abroad in the UK, the Netherlands, Germany, Hong Kong, Malaysia, or Thailand. There's an endless list of new adventures that await you in a UX career, even if you stay in your home country.

Like a lot of careers, there are typically two tracks as you grow: you can choose to remain as an "individual contributor," or you can go into the management track. The main difference between the two tracks is that individual contributors, or IC's, continue to contribute to research goals and projects regardless of their seniority.

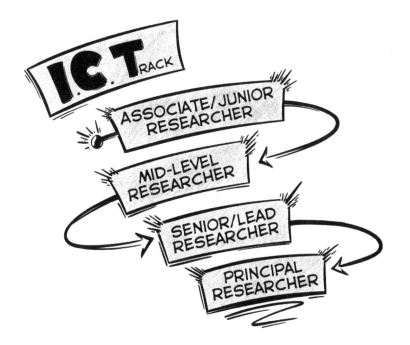

Those who transition into management certainly have more vertical opportunities, but they typically no longer contribute to "on the ground" day-to-day research tasks. Instead, they are more focused on the managerial and admin tasks of running and growing teams. When you first move into UX research, you will be an IC, either as a solo researcher or part of a team. If managing is something that's interesting to you later in your career, great. If not, also great! Either way, it's worthwhile to understand the potential pathways available to you when moving into a new field.

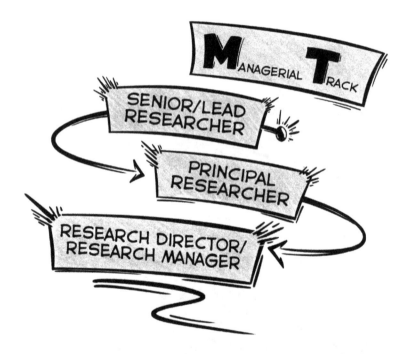

These are the rough career trajectories for the IC and managerial tracks. They vary from company to company, depending on the maturity of their research department and the size of the research teams.

Both career tracks offer a lot of personal and professional growth. The IC track gives you the opportunity to become an expert in the making-and-doing of research. The managerial track focuses on leadership and strategy. Many researchers move back and forth between the two tracks. At different points in your career, you might really enjoy becoming a subject matter expert and contributing to the daily research practice as an IC, or you may want to focus on growing a research team and elevating other researchers at your organization. I've found both to be incredibly satisfying during my years as a UX researcher.

As you read this book, keep these two options in the back of your mind, but don't focus on becoming a research manager in the next year. Spend the time to build your research foundation; it will serve you well in both an IC role and a managerial role if you decide to move into that career trajectory in the future.

There is a third trajectory of research consulting, but I do not recommend it for someone's first UX role. Consultants usually drop into a company for a specific project and a specific period of time. As a consultant, you will work as a solo researcher, often contracted by a company that does not have any in-house researchers on staff. Since consultants are self-employed, you are responsible for marketing yourself, finding jobs, and handling all the administrative and legal overhead of running your own one-person company. You will have to advocate hard for yourself and your research process, convincing folks at the company why your research is important for their business. You hand off the research at the end of a consulting project, but you don't stick around to see if or how the research is implemented. Some people find that dissatisfying, as you don't get to see the entire lifecycle of the work you produced.

If you are the type of person who loves to work for themselves and are interested in becoming a research consultant, I applaud you. It requires a special combination of marketing, entrepreneurial spirit, and independence that I do not have. The reason I don't recommend this type of position for someone's first research role is that you won't have the same mentorship or support structures built into an existing company. However, consulting on side projects can be a great way to cut your teeth and get some experience under your belt. How do you decide to do consulting? That depends on what makes the most sense for you. Are you comfortable learning things as you go and working independently, or would you prefer support and feedback from a team/manager?

WHAT TO EXPECT

Ok, so you have a sense of what the daily life and long-term career potentials are for UX research. Now let's get a sense of what to expect as you transition into the field. While researching this book, I interviewed many people about their experiences transitioning into UX and their perspectives on the field.

As a community, UX researchers have two contradicting but related beliefs about how to get into a research career:

UX research requires a specific degree

and

**Demonstrating real-life experience is
more important than a degree**

Before I dive into how it's even possible that UX research can hold both of these contradicting beliefs at the same time, let's explore each belief a little more.

UX research requires a specific degree

I've heard it from so many researchers: We don't want a degree to be a gatekeeper, but the reality is that lack of a degree often is a barrier to newer researchers breaking into the field. It's very difficult from my position as someone with a degree to say that I would've been able to get into UX research without it. I can say for certain that it helped, but it is probably impossible to parse how much of that assistance is from the experiences and methodology that I was able to translate into UX projects, and how much of it was the credential on the resume. Many of my colleagues at work have master-level or higher degrees, some in directly related research fields like anthropology and human factors. As someone who sits on hiring committees, a degree can be a useful, but overly simplistic, way to filter through stacks of resumes.

I can also say with certainty that I will never push a candidate forward based solely on a degree. I have said no to PhDs with decades of experience and yes to candidates with a year or less of "UX research" on their resume simply because they are able to talk about their process more effectively.

As companies become larger and their research teams grow, a few things can happen. One, the team can trend towards homogenization. In other words, the team can develop a culture of hiring only candidates from similar backgrounds. This can happen when hiring committees are biased, either intentionally or unintentionally, towards candidates that they "understand." When I see a resume with a background in anthropology, for instance, I have a good sense of the potential skill set and experiences that person can bring to the team before even meeting them. Though blunt, one of the safest methods of separating out those with more experience and those with less, is, unfortunately, to filter by degree. Or the organization might not be able to hire more junior team members for a variety of reasons, like contracting limitations, lack of managerial support, requirements for specific types of experience, and so on.

The second thing that can happen is that a team trends toward heterogeneity. It's risky hiring a future teammate if you aren't sure what their background offers in terms of training or skills. It's a big ask to take on mentoring junior teammates, especially if the senior-level members of the team wear many hats or aren't interested in a mentor role. For small teams, teams that move very quickly, or industries where research is held to very high standards, it's scary as a hiring manager to take on the challenge of growing a new researcher's skills up to par, potentially damaging your company's reputation in the process. There very simply might not be enough time for a senior person to support a more junior person with the necessary level of mentorship or oversight to help them grow. It's a special type of team or department that can make space for a range of expertise and provide the support needed in order for entry- and junior-level roles.

But please don't despair! If a degree in a research-related field is not something you have or are interested in getting, you shouldn't give up. The trick is to find a company that is heading towards heterogeneity, or a homogenous company if the team resembles you in terms of background. For instance, if you are applying to a company where you know many of the researchers have a background in cognitive science, and you have a background in cognitive science, leverage it! Seek out those companies! Look for hiring committees that will understand your experiences and know the value that you can bring to the team. When you're looking for jobs, heavily research the companies that you are applying to. LinkedIn is a great resource for this, especially since you can see who is employed at that company and what their backgrounds are. Google company blog posts or articles to get a sense of what projects they work on, and the backgrounds of the people they hire.

Even though we in the field are conflicted about needing blunt tools like a credential on a resume, most researchers come from non-traditional backgrounds, and this is still very much a part of the field's identity. At some point, we had to make the leap and market ourselves as capable of doing UX research. Perhaps that explains the second trend.

Demonstrating real-life experience is more important than having a degree.

So you don't have a degree in UX research-related fields. Maybe you get passed up by the companies who have to use a degree/no-degree filter. That's ok. Instead, you should look for a company that is more interested in hiring for practical skills. We'll talk more about how to find those types of jobs and companies in later chapters.

> "I have hired about 8-10 researchers so far, and having evaluated a lot of candidates, I can tell that there is a huge difference between what they learn in school and actual real-life knowledge that they can use."
>
> ZSOMBOR VARNAGY-TOTH

When hiring, I will happily choose a junior-level applicant who is able to articulate their research process and provide thoughtful, grounded answers over someone who has more experience but is unable to create a compelling story or provide justification for their research choices. Further, if I had to choose between two candidates with the same degree qualifications, I would go with the person who has valuable real-life experiences. Why?

As a researcher, your job is two-fold. You have to do the actual research, sure, and it needs to be grounded and as rigorous as possible given your constraints. But most importantly, that research has to mean something. It has to be actionable and easy for others to understand, but most importantly, you have to be able to communicate why it matters. Unlike academia, UX research for research's sake is meaningless. Theorizing for theory's sake does not ship a product, nor does it bring services to people in need. In order for your research to produce meaningful change, you need to be effective at bringing that research's story to life. Your job as a researcher will be to convince people who are in charge to bring the most benefit to your users.

"No one cares where you went to school. It's all about what you can do and can you prove it. Having that job experience is going to teach you in a way that school probably won't be able to."

ELIZABETH KAUFER

Our work as UX researchers is incredibly applicable to the real world, and our success hinges on our ability to deliver impactful recommendations. That's why having real-life experiences on your resume or in your portfolio is so critical. Show me what you are capable of instead of relying on a degree to tell me what you can do.

THEORIZING FOR THEORY'S SAKE DOES NOT SHIP A PRODUCT, NOR DOES IT BRING SERVICES TO PEOPLE IN NEED.

To sum this all up, researchers are able to hold these conflicting beliefs together because our work is so highly contextual. Yes, a person with a PhD might be the best candidate in a certain context, but a person without a graduate degree and more real-life experience could be the better candidate in a different context. UX research as a whole is very interested in not being proscriptive. This is why we feel conflicted when we say a degree matters, but promptly follow it up by saying, "but only when it matters".

Ok, so experience is more important than a degree, but how do you know you have the right kind of experience? The thing I hear most from people asking for my advice is, "I don't have any relevant experience." It's something I relate to at such a deep level, but it's the one belief that will absolutely prevent you from progressing into a UX research career. For that reason, it's the first belief we have to destroy. You will not become a researcher unless you dismantle the idea that your experiences and skills aren't applicable. The first step in your journey to becoming a UX researcher is to bolster your confidence in what you bring to the table.

> "People don't think that their skills are transferable. If they have deeply researched the migratory patterns of the blue heron, they think, 'That is all that I'm good for.' That's a mistake. There are people who have been managing their multinational PhD project for four years with assistants, with translators, and managing IRBs, but they say, 'I've never had a job.' I tell them, 'What do you mean? You're project managing right now!' The stumbling block that I see most often is people's inability to translate the skills into what are considered marketable."
>
> NICHOLE CARELOCK

In my previous life, I was an archaeologist, a healthcare worker, an outreach coordinator at a museum, a teaching assistant, a product manager. Notice that none of those roles have "UX" or "research" in their title! However, in each of these positions, I regularly interacted with people, learned about their challenges and struggles, and implemented programs or processes to better meet their needs. At some point in my career transition into UX, I had to translate the skills and responsibilities from my previous jobs into a package that said "researcher."

Here's what we're going to do now: grab a piece of paper or start a new notes doc on your computer. Let's call it your **Experience List**. Divide the list into three columns. On one side, list all the responsibilities, skills, and experiences you've had. Leave the second and third columns blank for now. You'll come back to the list at the end of the chapter, but first let's learn how to translate your previous experiences and skills.

Figuring out how to translate the skills you have into the language of another industry is hard. This is the point in your transition where you

need to start connecting where you've been to where you want to be.
It's your job at this point to start marketing yourself as a researcher.

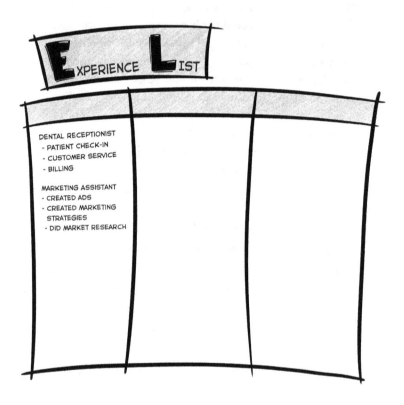

For example, most of my anthropological work involved writing eth-
nographies. During graduate school, I took a course where I was
embedded in a Somali community for four months as an after-school
tutor. At the end of the class, we submitted a report on a topic that
came up for us during our "tutor fieldwork"—I chose to study barriers
to vaccination among Somali children.

Here's how I would write an abstract on that work if I were publishing
or applying to an academic job:

I conducted a mid-term ethnography in the Seattle Somali community. Using Critical Theory approaches, I assessed the perception of vaccines, particularly the Measles Mumps Rubella (MMR), among children and mothers over the course of four months. My results demonstrate that misinformation campaigns about the safety of MMR vaccines have been particularly damaging to Somali groups due to a cultural belief that autism (a debunked but pervasively supposed side effect of the vaccine), especially among their male children, is a particular type of shame and burden on a family. I proposed recommendations that take into account culturally appropriate ways to address the safety and efficacy concerns of this population.

After reading this paragraph, I doubt your first thought was, "Ahhh, yes, she's a UX Researcher."

Now here is how I would present that same research for a UX position:

Over the course of four months, I conducted on-site research (contextual inquiries) and discovery interviews with Somali community members. My participants were children in after-school programs, their teachers, and the children's mothers. I discovered that:

- The community believes that vaccines aren't safe because of misinformation about their potential side effects

- Autism is heavily stigmatized in the Somali community, and the community believes that vaccines cause autism

- There is a deep fear and mistrust of doctors and vaccines in this community

- I recommend that any efforts to improve
  vaccination rates take into account these pain
  points. Potential solutions, such as information
  campaigns, should be tested with community
  members before they are rolled out to the larger
  community to make sure we are addressing the
  true concerns of community members.

What's the difference between the two? Look at the terms I used and the way I crafted my sentences. What's my tone? What's the focus of each? Which one is easier to read? Take a moment to think about a project you've completed and how you've talked about it. What would you change so that it's more digestible to a hiring committee looking for a UX candidate?

Now let's get back to the two examples. In the first example, I cite theoretical approaches and I refer to methods in academic terms (e.g., ethnography). I'm speaking to a very specific audience, one who understands the references I make to certain theories and methods.

In the second example, my language is plain and easier to parse. This is how a UX researcher would describe a study. In UX research, you call out who your users are. You might even justify why you included certain user groups. I don't focus on theoretical analysis, but on practical applications of the results. Instead of calling something a cultural barrier, I call it a pain point. I recommend that solutions follow tried-and-true UX research and product development processes: researching a problem and then testing a solution with a subset of the people who will use it before releasing it to the entire community.

The content of both examples is the same, but the audience is different. In the second example, I've translated it from something only an anthropologist could understand to something that is immediately understandable to a UX hiring committee. When you reframe your experiences, you aren't lying or diminishing your previous work. Instead, you're making it accessible.

It's critical to remember that my skills didn't change—the research experience that I have is the same whether I go with the first or second example. What changed is how I talk about it and how I demonstrate why that experience translates to UX work. You are building on the skills you learned in Step 0—you just need to practice talking about them! Moving past this mental block will be the biggest "Aha!" moment in your journey to getting a UX research position.

What experiences do you have that are specific to a type of job or field? How can you talk about that experience in a way that makes it understandable to someone who doesn't know anything about it? Come up with a few ideas or keywords and add them to the second column on your Experience List.

Speaking of your Experience List, let's start filling out those blank columns!

EXPERIENCE LIST EXERCISE

Your list is probably looking a little bare right now, but that's ok. At this point, you have a better sense of how to translate experiences, but that doesn't mean this will be an easy exercise, it might take a little soul-searching. When I did this exercise, it took me a while to see how my prior non-UX jobs or research could translate as "experience." I wasn't sure what counted or how to reframe experiences in a way that would explain why I wanted to move into UX.

So before we fill out the other columns, let's name them. Label column one **Past Experiences**, column two **UX Translation**, and column three **Why UX**. Your list should look something like this now:

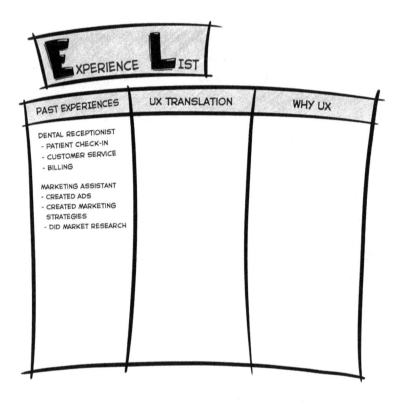

Before we dive into the **UX Translation** column, take a moment to think about why you want to become a UX researcher. What did you like (or not like) about your past jobs that makes you curious about UX research? For me, I loved listening to how people used websites or products and thinking up ways to improve them. The spark of inspiration you get when you come up with a solution that will solve a need is exhilarating, especially if the user didn't even realize they needed it! Spend a few minutes listing out why you want to do UX research in the **Why UX** column.

PAST EXPERIENCES	UX TRANSLATION	WHY UX
DENTAL RECEPTIONIST - PATIENT CHECK-IN - CUSTOMER SERVICE - BILLING MARKETING ASSISTANT - CREATED ADS - CREATED MARKETING STRATEGIES - DID MARKET RESEARCH		- I LIKE COMING UP WITH CREATIVE WAYS TO IMPROVE THE THINGS THAT PEOPLE USE - TOO MANY WEBSITES ARE HARD TO USE, I WANT TO MAKE IT EASIER FOR MORE PEOPLE - I ENJOY ANALYSING SURVEYS AND GETTING TO THE "WHY" - I'M CURIOUS, AND I DON'T GET TO USE MY CURIOSITY IN MY CURRENT JOB THE WAY I'D LIKE

Reminding yourself why you're doing this will ground how you translate your past experiences, and it's a useful exercise for later chapters when we get into writing cover letters and interviewing for jobs.

Now it's time to dive into the **UX Translation** column. This is where you'll need to remember the specifics about your previous roles. Let's say you did patient check-in as a dental receptionist, but what about how you listened to patient complaints and overhauled the check-in processes so that patients didn't wait as long? That's a UX project! In that same role, you sent out monthly patient satisfaction surveys, because the dentist wanted to know what could be improved. You analyzed all those surveys and realized that patients really hated the music in the waiting room because it made them anxious before a root canal. (Your previous dentist boss had a thing for Swedish death metal). So you petitioned the dentist to change the station to something more friendly and upbeat, and next month's satisfaction scores went way up!

At your previous marketing job, you managed the market research where you would talk to a few customers after they finished shopping. The insights you got from these conversations changed the marketing ad strategy for the company, and you used those conversations to test different versions of ads to see which was most appealing to customers.

Your past experiences might not match these examples, but you can see how something simple like "I did market research" or "I sent patient satisfaction surveys" can be translated into a UX research experience line on your resume!

Continue filling out the **UX Translation** column. Each translation doesn't have to be perfect! Just get the translations onto paper for now—we'll come back to your Experience List when we build out your resume and portfolio in Chapter 3.

WHAT TO READ NOW

iwantauxjob.com/chapter2

Herminia Ibarra, Working Identity

Carrie Boyd, "The State of User Research Report 2018"

Nielson Norman Group, "Research Methods Cheatsheet"

Nielson Norman Group, "Usability Testing 101"

Guide to User Research UXR

ELIZABETH'S UX STORY

Elizabeth Kaufer

Elizabeth is a senior UX researcher at a government contracting firm where she works on federal healthcare projects. She has extensive experience working in a range of UX roles. Despite her many graduate degrees, she and I talked at length about her thoughts on the necessity of a master's or PhD and the complicated benefits of professional standards in the field.

What does a day in the life of a researcher look like for you?

It involves a lot of typical stuff you'll see UX researchers doing: conducting UX research, specifically qualitative research, designing research plans, writing tests, writing conversation guides, interviewing and performing usability testing with stakeholders and with users, analyzing those results and then putting them into a format that will convince stakeholders to do what we think is important to do. There's a lot of cross-collaboration, too. I work most closely with other folks in the UX space, but we also collaborate with people in stakeholder positions, in development, and in product and project management. Basically, people that have a stake in how this project is going to actually get done.

In my company, there are also a lot of opportunities to work with other researchers to make our research processes better. For example, if I want to run an unmoderated usability test, how should I do that? We want those guides for our company so that we deliver a consistent product.

How did you know you wanted to do UX research? What got you interested in the field?

After being in the working world for a couple of years, I realized that the work I was doing wasn't what I wanted to be doing forever. I looked at my work experience in the museum space and education, and I realized I'm a person who loves learning, problem-solving, and user advocacy. I really like helping people figure things out and figuring out what they think and do. That's why I decided to go back to grad school at Pratt for Library and Information Science because I want to make things easy for a group of people to find information or to accomplish a task.

Originally I wanted to be an academic librarian, but early on I saw an alum talk about his job as a user experience designer and I thought "that sounds awesome, I want to do that." Pratt has courses on user experience in their curriculum, and you can specialize in UX as a concentration, so that was my introduction to UX research.

And you went back and got another graduate degree?

Sure did. While the curriculum for my second degree had practical elements, like learning new research methods and research skills, it was more focused on bigger, academic questions. My second graduate experience in Internet Studies at Oxford wasn't necessarily "let's make sure at the end of this you have a really great portfolio that you can use to get a job." It was "let's make sure that you can do a rigorous academic research study that could be published."

I would not say that I needed my second degree to be a successful UX researcher, but it definitely informed a lot of my experience and research skills. It had a positive impact, but it's not a requirement for being successful in this area.

What made you want to get that degree, given that you say you don't think it's a requirement?

A lot of the questions we talked about in my library science degree were about the impact that technology has on all parts of

society. Those questions were really fascinating and really excit-
ing, and I wanted to explore them more.

**What do you think it means for the field and for more
junior people who are getting into this industry?**

I do think it is a good thing—having professional standards
does matter. When people do the work badly, it unfortunately
impacts the field as a whole. There's a reason that academic journals are really rigorous in who gets to become part of the canon.
If you have just any person writing any old silly thing without
any standards, it undermines the field's credibility. In that sense,
those professional standards are a good thing.

But I appreciate that it does make it harder when you're new.
When hiring, we don't consider people who don't have a certain
kind of work experience or certain kind of training, but at the
end of the day, that's true of many jobs. And that's not necessarily a bad thing. We want people to be doing this work well, especially because our work involves human beings who are placing
a lot of trust in us. We want to be thoughtful, careful, and professional. The decisions we make based on the research we do
will to impact all the people that use our technology. So we do
want to have a field that has ethics, that has standards.

For those folks that are trying to get into it UX, focus on getting practical experience. If you were going into UX now, you'd
want to find a program that gives you important foundational
skills and methods, but also gives you those opportunities to
prove it in real-world situations. This is a thing that you hear
about a lot from people in all jobs: that no one cares where you
went to school, it's all about what you can prove you can do.
But if you're new to the UX field, you need to learn how to do it
and you need to have an environment where you can prove it;

formal schooling is one way for that to happen. Having something that demonstrates you understand what it means to do UX research in a practical and strategic sense, like a portfolio, is a huge asset.

3

FINDING YOUR COMMUNITY

I can't stress enough how important it is to find a community while you're going through this process of becoming a UX researcher. A community of mentors and peers will help you track and assess your growth, provide you with inspiration, and serve as a sounding board for your ideas and concerns.

A good support network will help you grow your skills and confidence as a researcher. These might include Meetup groups, UX-related social groups or Facebook pages, conferences, or formal mentorships. These are incredibly useful venues for entering UX research, becoming part of the community, and growing in your career.

The Mixed Methods Slack channel is singlehandedly one of the best resources on the internet. It's a UX researcher community with channels for nearly every city in the US, a channel for finding a mentor, and an excellent jobs channel, which is where I found my first UX researcher role. If you do nothing else, join that group*.

EPIC and UXPA are two professional organizations that also throw annual conferences, which are widely attended and offer an excellent avenue for networking, learning from different fields, and finding jobs. They host workshops at their conferences, which cover professional development topics like interviewing, writing better resumes, or building portfolios.

Not only are these communities often where the best jobs are shared first, but they are thriving resources for any sort of research-related question, from how to find a job to how to convince reluctant stakeholders.

Real talk: it can be terrifying breaking into a new community, especially when you are changing careers or starting in a new field. UX research overall is an incredibly welcoming space, because so many of us have come to UX from a winding path. The UX research community is incredibly welcoming. I was surprised at how welcoming when I first started reaching out. My first mentor was someone I met through a Ladies Who UX meetup in DC. After a few others in the meetup expressed interest in creating a "learn how to become a researcher workgroup," she hosted us at her house every Friday for a few weeks and took time out to give us feedback on our workgroup projects.

Overwhelmingly, folks in this field are open, accommodating, and happy to spend an hour or so with you over coffee as you pepper them with questions about the field and how to get a job. When I was first starting out, people were happy to put in a word at a company for me, read over a resume, or suggest a new book or resource. UX researchers,

---

* To join Mixed Methods Slack group go to www.mixed-methods.org

perhaps by nature of being empathetic and interested in helping others, have built an incredibly rich community of care.

But how do you find this community? If you live in a bigger city or a city with a large tech industry, UX research and UX design events are common. Go to events, be open and curious, and meet people. Tell people you're looking to break into the field, practice reframing your experiences in more UX-researcher ways, and ask if it resonates. Aim to have one or two solid connections from each event, and ask if they'd be up for coffee or a phone call in the future where you can pick their brain on UX research and how they got into the field. People love to talk about themselves!

If you live in a smaller town or a city without a large tech scene, don't despair. The online community of UX researchers is well-developed and just as welcoming as those in person. Get familiar with cold-emailing people through LinkedIn, do virtual coffees, and see if there are any local university or college-based UX programs you could join. (Side note: research is increasingly remote-work friendly, so even if you don't want to move, you can still find UX positions!)

Joining these groups is great for professional growth and exposing yourself to new opportunities, but it's also how you can start to feel like a part of the research community. That will go a long way towards helping you feel more and more like a researcher yourself.

Here are some ideas on groups to seek out, or places to start when looking for people to do "virtual coffee" with. I also highly recommend joining these groups and professional organizations as you transition into UX research:

- Company-sponsored events for researchers, like a Google UX Research hangout

- Conferences like UXPA, Convey UX, Design Thinking, CHI, IXDA, or EPIC
- Local UX Research association like UXPA, which has chapters in most US and international cities and EPIC
- Community college or university student research groups
- Facebook groups
    Tech Ladies
    UX Researchers Association
    Association of Internet Researchers (AoIR)
    User Research Collective
- LinkedIn groups
    UXPA International
    User Experience Group
    User Experience
- Reddit forums
    r/userexperience
    r/UXResearch

Not only will a community help your grow your network, which is very useful in the job search, it will also provide you with an arena to practice your skills as a researcher, learn the culture of the work (how other researchers talk about their work, how they interact with each other), and get a sense of the local job market (where are good fits, where should you avoid applying to). It will also serve as a north star for your potential career growth. A community will provide you with role models as well as peers and provide support as you reinvent yourself as a researcher.

Undoubtedly, you'll find others who know exactly what you are going through during this transition. If possible, find a mentor who has a similar background to you. Ask them if they would be up for a thirty-minute chat every few weeks while you work on your portfolio and resume and apply for jobs. A mentor with the same experiences as you can assist you in crafting your story and framing your background. (This is where your Experience List can come in handy!)

While UX folks are generally very open to helping, do recognize that you are asking for a fair amount of time and emotional energy, so be respectful of that and focus on maximizing your time with them. Be prepared with a few questions that are specific and show that you've done some homework. Here's an example of how to reach out to someone:

> Hi [Their Name],
>
> I read your article about UX research and robots recently, and I noticed on your LinkedIn profile that you have a background in economics. I also have an economics degree, and I'm in the process of moving into a UX research career. I'd love to get your thoughts on how you leveraged your economics background when you moved into UX research. Would you be up for a quick 30-minute chat sometime next week?
>
> Best,
> [Your Name]

Once you've arranged a chat with them, craft a few questions or themes that you want their opinion on. Great questions could include things like, "I'm interested in how you went about finding jobs in your city" or "How did you frame your experience as an accountant?" Avoid really general questions like "What is UX research?"—such broad questions will lead to less actionable insights from the answer.

Later on, once you've found a career as a UX researcher, pay it forward!

WHAT TO READ OR LISTEN TO NOW

iwantauxjob.com/chapter3

UX Beginners "Top UX Communities & Groups"

Dollars to Donuts Podcast by Steve Portigal

MANDY'S UX STORY

Mandy Lee is a UX researcher at a research and design agency. As someone who has only recently gotten into UX, she has a valuable perspective on how to translate your experiences and get your first UX role.

Tell me about how you got started as a researcher. What has been your career path?

I've worked at various industries as a behavior therapist for kids with autism, marketing, and HR before I transitioned to UX research. To learn more about the UX world, I started reaching out to people I didn't know with a UX Researcher title on LinkedIn, asking for advice and what their day-to-day looks like. Then I started attending local meetups to network and meet with people over coffee. During this process, I was taking several online classes, reviewing people's research portfolios, and reading lots of books. Finally, I worked on a couple of independent projects to put my portfolio together. Then I found an opportunity at my current company. I started working on my transition on October 2018 and got my job in June 2019.

What do you wish you could tell past-you when you first got started as a researcher?

To not worry and be more patient.

What are some stumbling blocks that people getting into research might experience?

Many people might think that they have zero experience or skills that can be applied as a UX researcher, but we interact with people every day, just like researchers do all the time. You can find transferrable skills that can be applied as a UX researcher— some of those skills you might need to practice and get more experience, but you can grow from there. It's hard to get your very first job "without any experience," but it just takes some creative thinking. Work with other people, like UX designers, on a project together, or reach out to small businesses to inform them about UX research and how valuable it is and offer to work on a small project. I think you just have to be very proactive and persistent.

What do you think makes a good researcher?

Always being curious and able to advocate for users and deliver their empathy!

HOW TO CRAFT
A RESUME

This chapter is about how to sell yourself on paper. The following information will apply whether this is your first job out of college or are transitioning careers into UX. The way you craft your cover letter and resume is critical because it's the first introduction a hiring committee has to you, your skills, and what you can add to their company. Your resume and cover letter are first impressions, so make sure they convey your full experience. It is also important to curate your skill set specifically for each job. Remember, it's not uncommon to have several versions of a resume and cover letter so you can tailor it for each job application.

Before diving into how to craft a resume specifically for UX, let's go over the Do's and Don'ts for resumes. Yes, some of these suggestions are generic to all resumes, but I've seen a lot of bad UX resumes. If your fundamentals aren't good, the specific advice won't help.

Do

- Speak to specifics rather than generals

    E.g., Recruited over 100 users for 10+ studies over six months vs. Recruited users

- Include metrics where possible

    E.g., My recommendations increased sales by 25% vs Made recommendations that increased sales

- Be consistent with verb tense and tone

    E.g., Keep all past job responsibilities verbs in past tense and current job description in present tense

- Include portfolio links!

Put your portfolio on a hiring committee's radar at the beginning of the hiring process! This helps the hiring committee understand how you approach and present your research, and it gives a fuller picture of who you are as a candidate. Including a portfolio in your application could be the difference between them choosing between you and another candidate.

Don't

- Include your high school graduation date

    You did not peak in high school. Ageism is real— a hiring committee might unconsciously think you are too young or too old for this role. Rarely will listing high school information add anything to who you are as a candidate, so better to leave it off your resume completely.

- Include everything

    Only include the experiences that speak to your research skills and potential. Remember, a resume is not a CV. One to two pages (max) is all you should need. Your future recruiters and hiring managers will thank you.

- Assume a job title or degree tells the whole story

    Not every recruiter or hiring manager understands what a psychology or economics degree means in practical terms for a UX role. Make your resume your first example of UX research and design in practice: tailor it to the needs of your users—the people who will read it and hire you based on it. What do they need to see to be convinced that you are the right candidate?

- Sell yourself short

    Only worked a few years before going back to school? First job out of college? Doesn't matter. You have experience. College projects are portfolio projects. The two years you spent as a research assistant in undergrad counts as professional experience. Be confident in what you bring to the table.

- Succumb to design trends

    There's no need to overly design your resume. A machine-readable, text-based document format is preferable to a highly stylized resume done in Illustrator. (Note: if you are seeking a designer role, you might want to show off design skills via your resume, but is not necessary for most research roles.)

Now let's get into the nitty-gritty of framing your resume for a UX position. First, we'll learn how to frame your experiences to connect to a UX role in general, and then how to frame your experiences and curate your resume for a particular job description.

HOW TO FRAME
YOUR RESUME FOR UX

I can't emphasize strongly enough how much you should approach your resume as a UX research project. Think of your resume as a research deliverable. Your users are those who will read your resume: recruiters, hiring managers, future colleagues, company executives. What do they need to know to move you forward to an interview? This is where informational interviews can really help you out. If you have a sense of the culture of the company or research sector that you are applying for, you can tailor your resume content to exactly what they want to hear to be convinced that you are the best applicant for the job.

What are the user needs of a recruiter?

Most recruiters are not experts in the fields that they recruit for. In other words, a recruiter will not know everything about what makes a good researcher. What they know, however, is what the company wants to see in a candidate. They will have a list of keywords (or at least a list of qualities) they're looking for, and that's how they will sort through the stacks of resumes they receive. Your job is to make the recruiter's job easy: concisely and clearly point out the keywords that matter for that role. Use words that demonstrate your research experience. Recruiters are interested in job titles and responsibilities that match the keywords on their list.

Here's an example of a line on a resume tailored so it makes immediate sense to a recruiter. I added formatting to emphasize the structure of the content, but it's not necessary in an actual resume:

FIELD ASSISTANT

- conducted **contextual inquiries** with *three field sites*

- **designed research plan and conversation guide** for *research participants*

- **recruited three field sites** to participate in the study, *exceeded study goal by two sites*

- **analyzed data and reported results** to *field site directors*

- **recommended record keeping changes** that resulted in *30% more efficient laboratory operating procedures*

What this tells the recruiter

If I was a recruiter reading this resume, I wouldn't have to read between the lines—you've clearly described research methods, participant recruitment, and how you accomplished more than expected. I don't need to search for keywords or guess what you mean by certain duties, since there's a clear what you did, how you did it, and who you did it with or for. I can see what you did without being an expert in UX research. I know that this type of experience is attractive to the hiring committee because they gave me a list of what to look for in a resume.

Here's an example of the same resume but without specifics:

FIELD ASSISTANT

- Participated in visits to sites

- Point person for site visits

- Asked questions on standard operating procedures

- Created research reports

- Proposed recommendations

- Wrote standard operating procedures

What this tells the recruiter

Not much. If I were a recruiter, I wouldn't see any of the keywords my hiring committee asked me to read for (like what types of participants you worked with, what methods you used, what impact you had). Aside from knowing you visited sites, I have no idea what you did as a field assistant. I have 300 more resumes to sort through today and twenty interviews to schedule. I need to immediately understand who you are and what you bring to the table. I don't have the domain knowledge to read between the lines here.

What are the needs of the hiring committee?

It's very likely that you will be interviewing with your potential future colleagues, often on your immediate team. You need to understand what their needs are. What skills are they looking for? What skills are they missing on the team? This is where LinkedIn, public research, or personal connections to the company come in handy. Say you know someone on the team has the same background as you, or you find a blog post by the team manager about how they like to use personas.

This information not only tells you something about what they want to hear, but also how to frame your experiences. If you know that the director is looking for someone to round out their data analytic skills for the team, make sure to emphasize your experience with analyzing large datasets. Aside from an understanding of research methods and skills, a hiring committee is also looking for a culture fit. Will you collaborate and take direction well? How will you contribute to the growth of the team and the company culture? Speak to this in your resume and cover letter.

GOOD

- Self-employed researcher
- Worked as a sole researcher supporting several

teams across multiple companies, including Fortune 500 like X, Y, and Z and small businesses like A, B, and C

- Collaboratively designed studies with company designers, product managers, and senior stakeholders

- Planned and facilitated workshops, which resulted in company adopting new on-boarding procedures, increasing new employee satisfaction by 45%

What this tells a hiring manager

You've explicitly told me that you've worked across teams with a variety of other disciplines. This means it's probably safe to hire you in a role that needs to work across a lot of different teams in order to be successful. You talked about novel strategies that I might want to incorporate in my company, such as workshops (which no one on my team has experience with). That makes you an interesting addition to the team's skill set. As a sole researcher, that tells me you know how to manage your time and can work independently, but you have also worked a great deal in a collaborative environment. Best of both worlds!

LESS GOOD

- Self-employed researcher
- Worked as sole researcher
- Designed research studies
- Conducted workshops

What this tells a hiring manager

Who did you work with? What was your experience as a sole researcher? What sort of studies did you design? How were your workshops perceived? This resume would leave me with more questions than answers.

Since I have twenty more resumes to read through, this would get sorted into the "no" pile.

HOW TO FRAME YOUR
RESUME FOR A SPECIFIC JOB

Let's start with a generic UX research job description, which I created from an amalgamation of job listings I pulled from a job board site.

Company ABC is looking for an enthusiastic, entry- to mid-level researcher who will contribute to the team's delivery of high-quality, user-centered designs and products.

JOB DUTIES:

- Collect information to analyze and evaluate existing or proposed functionality across a variety of platforms (e.g., desktop, smartphone, tablet, interactive store displays, POS devices)

- Plan, conduct, and report on UX research

- Partner closely with Design and Product to ensure that solutions are customer-centric

- Partner with Marketing and Sales to understand business priorities and frame research questions to deliver lasting business value

- Work closely with other researchers, data scientists, and marketing research to develop a holistic understanding of the data

- Generate actionable UX research insights to drive customer-centric decision-making with stakeholders

- Proactively and routinely surface fact-based, forward-thinking customer insights across business partnerships

QUALIFICATIONS:

- 3-5 years experience with research, design research, product research or equivalent
- Thorough understanding of research methodologies, including usability testing, heuristic evaluations, and information architecture
- Experience with mobile design preferred
- Demonstrated ability to work with tight deadlines
- Able to work collaboratively across teams

Let's say that you are interested in applying for this job. First, let's learn how to read for what they want in the ideal candidate.

How to read a job description

Understanding what a company wants from their job description often feels like more of an art than a skill. Sometimes companies have their own unique styles of writing job descriptions, and there are numerous articles on how to decipher them. Emily Stevens, UX Designer and Managing Editor at CareerFoundry, an online learning platform, wrote a great introduction on how to understand UX-related job descriptions*. Emily's article is focused on UX designer jobs, but she has a short section on what you can expect to see in a UX research role. (I've listed her article in the end-of-chapter resources if you want to give it a deeper read.)

There are three big takeaways that are relevant to what we're learning in this chapter. The first is to think of the years of experience in the job ad as a rough guideline. Two-to-three years of experience might be junior at one company, but mid-level at another. Instead of focusing on whether you have those two-to-three years of experience, focus

---

* Emily Stevens "A Guide To UX Designer Job Descriptions: How To Write And Interpret Them" careerfoundry.com/en/blog/ux-design/ux-designer-job-descriptions-guide/)

on if the job will be the right fit for where you are in your growth as a researcher. You should also keep in mind the different titles and levels of experience required for those titles in different settings. A mid-level researcher at a large tech company might require more years of experience and a more developed skill set than a senior-level researcher at a small startup.

Second, use the skills and responsibilities listed in the job posting to understand what research means to that company. Look at your Experience List—does the role seem like it would be a good fit based on your past experiences? Does it seem like the job would help you grow in the skills that you want to strengthen?

How will you know if it's a good fit? Scan the job description for what types of words they are using. Do they use usability testing a lot? What methods do they explicitly call out? Are there preferred skills or training they ask for? Let's practice the same job posting as an example:

Company ABC is looking for an enthusiastic, **entry- to mid-level researcher** who will contribute to the team's delivery of high-quality, user-centered designs and products.

JOB DUTIES:

- Collect information to analyze and evaluate existing or proposed functionality across a **variety of platforms** (e.g., desktop, smartphone, tablet, interactive store displays, POS devices)

- Plan, conduct, and report on UX research

- Partner closely with Design and Product to ensure that solutions are customer-centric

- Partner with Marketing and Sales to understand business priorities and frame research questions to **deliver lasting business value**

- Work closely with other researchers, data scientists and marketing research to develop a holistic understanding of the data

- Generate actionable UX research insights to **drive customer-centric decision-making with stakeholders**

- **Proactively surface** fact-based, forward-thinking **customer insights across business partnerships**

QUALIFICATIONS:

- **3-5 years experience** with research, design research, product research or equivalent

- Thorough understanding of research methodologies, including **usability testing, heuristic evaluations, and information architecture.**

- Experience with mobile design preferred

- Demonstrated ability to work with tight deadlines

- Able to **work collaboratively across teams**

By pulling out just the bolded items from above, we can glean the type of candidate that this company is looking for.

Who: Entry- to mid-level

What this means: This is the perfect position for someone starting out. The fact that they are calling this out shows me they are not expecting to interview senior-level candidates or looking for someone with 20+ years of experience. This level-sets what kind of peer candidates you'll be judged against.

What: Someone who can work collaboratively with a variety of other teams (like marketing, research, design, product) and across products and platforms (desktop, mobile, etc.). The ideal candidate sounds like someone who is able to advocate for change by generating meaningful insights into the customer's needs, therefore creating lots of business value (aka money for the company).

What this means: Highlight the experiences that show you know how to deliver value. Tell your stories about big (or small) changes you made in previous roles or research projects that had an impact. Your stories don't necessarily need to be related to money or products. Maybe you proposed recommendations to your university's website that resulted in 15% more minorities entering engineering degrees. Perhaps you offered changes to your company's on-boarding process that increased employee satisfaction and length of tenure by 75%. Maybe the insights from your usability research during college courses helped your project team reduce user frustration with the app you prototyped. Drive home how you affect change, be it small or large, and connect that to the work you could do if hired.

How: Usability tests, heuristics, information architecture, collaborative work

What this means: Whenever possible, use the keywords in the job description in your resume and cover letter. Talk about your experiences working on a team or across many teams, even if it isn't related to UX research. Be sure to call out any experiences or portfolio pieces that show your expertise with the methods they explicitly referred to. Even better, explicitly select any portfolio pieces or work stories that involve usability tests, running a heuristic analysis, or improving information architecture.

Another trick when reading job descriptions is to look at phrases. "Hard skills" (e.g., specific methods) can be picked out of the job description directly. In the example above, they explicitly call out usability tests, for instance, and experience designing across various platforms. Phrases such as "work collaboratively across teams" are used to describe "soft skills," which are used to figure out culture fit. It's a good idea to weave both hard and soft skills into your resume and your cover letter, but you can let your resume emphasize the hard skills. Since your cover letter lends itself well to a narrative format, it's a great place to highlight your soft skills.

The last takeaway from Emily's article is the variety of specialist roles that you will see in UX job listings. UX Copywriter, UX Strategist, UX Design Researcher, and UX Information Architect are likely to pop up during your job search. UX Researcher is one of many specialist roles that fall under the umbrella of UX. Some of these roles are natural gateways to UX research, while others are more specialized versions of design or research that you can grow into as you gain more experience. We'll talk more about how you can leverage these roles to get your first UX position in Chapter Five.

Now that we've talked about what to look for, it's time to talk about what to avoid. Jamal Nichols, another UX designer who's site Truth About Design teaches you how to transition into a UX design career, wrote a great Medium post calling out examples of bad UX job descriptions and why you want to avoid them*. Jamal's article is a great counterpoint to Emily's, because it tells you exactly what you don't want to see in a job description! Like Emily, Jamal focuses on UX design jobs, but there's a lot that is relevant to research roles as well. His article is listed at the end of the chapter, and I highly recommend reading it so you only spend your time applying for jobs that you actually want and are a good fit for you. Some highlights from his article are to avoid jobs with overly

---

* Jamal Nichols "Terrible UX Design Job Descriptions (Or: How To Avoid Bad UX Design Jobs)" medium.com/truthaboutdesign/terrible-ux-design-job-descriptions-or-how-to-avoid-bad-ux -design-jobs-c254ba23b7eb

flowery language, run from roles that ask you for "code designs," and say no to jobs with reporting structures that don't make sense.

Jamal is right to say that UX designers should be wary of jobs that ask them to code. UX research has a similar red flag, and it's to be wary of job descriptions that ask for a blended designer/researcher. There are lots of designers who can research well, and there are lots of researchers who have quite the artistic eye, but the two fields are specialized for a reason. It takes a unique type of person to do each job well. If the job posting asks for a researcher who can also build prototypes, that probably means that the company either 1) doesn't understand that the two jobs are different, or 2) does understand that they are different but only have the budget to hire one person. In the second situation, you might have a cash-strapped company that recognizes the value of research but desperately needs someone who can build, too. If you don't already have a strong design background, I would not recommend a hybrid designer/researcher role to someone starting out as a researcher as there's a lot to learn to do both design and research well on their own. At some point in your research career path, it might make sense to branch out and grow your skills as a designer or other UX specialist role. But for now, focus on the research foundations and landing your first research job.

Another red flag for research jobs is when the job description doesn't call out keywords that you would expect to see for a research-focused role. This indicates two things. One, that the company does not have a mature research practice; otherwise they would've had a researcher on staff to consult with when writing a job description for hiring additional researchers. You generally won't find a lot of support at this kind of company, so consider if that is important for you to have in your first research role. Two, this could indicate that the company is large enough to have thoroughly standardized all their job postings. Big tech companies are notorious for non-descript job postings. In that case, find other researchers at that company and ask them about their typical responsibilities to get a sense of what the company is looking for in a researcher, because you won't find it in their job description.

TAILORING YOUR EXPERIENCE TO A JOB DESCRIPTION

So let's say the job description passes the smell test and is a good fit for you. Now it's time to tailor your experiences to that job description. This is your opportunity to highlight the hard and soft skills that you think the company wants to see.

Imagine that as part of your academic or previous career work, you helped a local non-profit design a mobile app to improve the literacy outcomes of Pre-K students. This is how you might describe that work in a resume:

RESEARCHER, COMMUNITY LITERACY NON-PROFIT, 2011-2014

- Conducted three years of ethnographic research with low-income communities in Minnesota
- Created an early education program, designed in collaboration with community members and local stakeholders
- Researched community needs to inform the design of a mobile-friendly app to introduce literacy to pre-K students
- Designed research plan and conversation guide to test the usability and heuristics of the mobile-friendly app
- Recruited ten community members and five Pre-K students for usability tests

- Conducted two rounds of usability testing on mobile app

- Provided recommendations on app design to increase usability scores by 10 points

I included a number of points that relate directly to what's listed in the job description:

- Three-to-five years of experience with research

- Demonstrated knowledge of research methodologies and lifecycle: recruiting users, usability testing, information architecture

- Experience with mobile design (mobile app)

- Emphasis on collaborative nature of work: dealing with stakeholders, balancing community needs, providing recommendations based on research

Now that you have a sense of how to talk about your job experience, how do you build the rest of your resume? This is where you can get creative. Focus on the things that make you unique as a candidate. Do you have certain skills that are hard to come by? For example, if you speak several languages, list them with your level of fluency. Do you know Photoshop and Illustrator? Do you know enough coding languages to be dangerous? Emphasize specialized software that's relevant to the job and avoid filling a skills section with every single program you know. Since most folks in the tech industry know how to use Microsoft Word, it's not worth listing on your resume.

Optimize your precious one-to-two pages worth of text to really drive home who you are as a candidate. Be concise, be impactful. Every line needs to deliver at least one meaningful idea. Edit and copyedit viciously. Have friends and colleagues proofread it. Have someone who works in UX do a gut-check it (see Chapter 2 - Finding your community). And never get too attached—a resume should be a living document that grows alongside you.

Here's an example using my current resume.

Lauryl Zenobi
○ lauryl@iwantauxjob.com ○ Resume and portfolio at laurylzenobi.com ○

Professional experience

Senior UX Researcher
AD HOC, LLC   *June 2018–present*

- Working with the Department of Veterans Affairs to improve veteran services and VA employee tools
- Research lead for a human centered design team of researchers and a designer
- Trained and mentored two junior researchers
- Contributes to business development and Research Practice Area development

UX Researcher
AD HOC, LLC   *Aug 2017–June 2018*

- Worked with CMS to improve digital services and modernize legacy systems for hospitals reporting quality of care data
- I designed, moderated, and analyzed research sessions with >150 CMS system users, while helping to develop and direct a HCD research process for CMS' Hospital Quality Reporting system

AnthroGuide Product Manager
AMERICAN ANTHROPOLOGICAL ASSOCIATION   *Feb 2016–Aug 2017*

- Spearheaded a user-centered overhaul of the AnthroGuide database, resulting in improved UX and functionality of AnthroGuide website
- Updated layout of AnthroGuide to decrease cognitive load and increase database accessibility and functionality
- Implemented new pricing informed by user research, increasing sales
- Conducted interviews and surveys to assess pain-points and accessibility, involving >200 users, synthesized user research to identify areas of improvement
- Managed >$280k sales revenue, increased sales by >$50k and 22% during tenure

Education
2016   MA Archaeology (PhD candidate), UNIVERSITY *of* WASHINGTON
2011   BA Anthropology, UNIVERSITY *of* HAWAII *at* HILO

Professional membership
UXPA, Seattle Chapter
American Anthropological Association

Skillset
Usability testing, qualitative research and design, data synthesis, persona development, wireframes, user-flows, HTML5/CSS3, Git, WordPress, Sketch, Balsamiq, UXPin, Keynote, Proto.io, Marvel, Omnigraffle, Adobe suite, CorelDraw, Canva, CMS, Tableau, R statistical software.

The last thing to consider is your cover letter. Are cover letters important? Early on in your career transition, yes. A good cover letter will never hurt, but not including one in your job application might.

I generally tailor a resume to a job before writing a cover letter, which helps me organize the key experiences that I want to highlight in my application. Follow the same Do's and Don'ts for your cover letter as for your resume. Your cover letter is a narrative version of your resume. Write clearly and include keywords and phrases from the job description. Keep it short and to the point, one page or less, but include some of your personality. This is where you can add color, detail, and more metrics to the experiences you list in your resume. Use your cover letter to drive home why you are interested in UX research and how your experiences will translate well to the role.

HOW DO YOU KNOW
YOU'RE QUALIFIED?

It can be really intimidating to read over job descriptions that ask for five-plus years of experience in a field that you are just transitioning into. However, you probably are more qualified than you think. Any time you spent during your undergrad or graduate work doing research with users counts as experience! You don't need to have a UX researcher title on your resume to get a UX research position. If you are working on side projects to build out your UX portfolio, that counts as experience! Are you implementing UX research methods in your current job, even if your job is doing something unrelated to UX research? That's experience! Count those as years when looking over a job description and write your cover letter to that effect.

I love Emily's emphasis on not focusing too much on years of experience. You may have ten years of work experience but that doesn't necessarily make you qualified for a Senior Researcher role that requires ten years of research experience. Years of experience won't be a one-to-one match since there are other aspects of being a UX researcher you can only learn on the job. You might have five years of graduate work under your belt and find you are being offered an entry-level research position. This is humbling, but it's a start. As someone starting out in the field, a fancy title is much less important than finding a work environment that is supportive and provides room for you to grow as a researcher.

The company that hires you cares just as much that the role is a good fit for you. As someone who hires other researchers, I want to know that my company can provide them with the right level of support. There's nothing worse than hiring someone at a level that isn't a good match for their skills. This does a huge disservice to the new employee and can also negatively impact the company as a whole. It's often better to hire someone at a more junior level knowing they'll be able to outperform expectations and quickly rise to a senior level.

Regardless if you're hired at a mid- or entry-level research position, always advocate for what you deserve at that level! Negotiate pay, verify that you will have professional development opportunities, and make sure the team is a good culture fit for you. Just because you're switching fields doesn't mean you should be grateful for whatever job comes across your plate. Be humble and acknowledge that you have lots of room to grow in your new role, but maintain your confidence in your skills and what you can bring to a team.

WHAT TO READ NOW

iwantauxjob.com/chapter4

Emily Stevens, "A Guide To UX Designer Job Descriptions: How To Write And Interpret Them"

Jamal Nichols, "Terrible UX Design Job Descriptions (Or: How To Avoid Bad UX Design Jobs)"

NICHOLE'S UX STORY

Nichole Carelock

Nichole is a principal researcher and digital strategy director who works with the Federal government. We learned a little bit about her start in UX research in the Introduction.

I spoke with Nichole about her process of moving into UX research after finishing up a postdoc in anthropology. She has an incredible perspective on the identity shift that can happen as you leave behind previous career paths for UX research. She also has many valuable ideas on how to approach building out your resume and portfolio in a way that is authentic to your skill set.

What was applying to jobs like for you?

One of the hardest things that I did on my resume was to take out my academic experience. To say, "Ok, you've shown what you've read, right? You've shown what you've written. But how can we highlight what you've done?"

One of the most useful things for me was to take out the theoretical application of knowledge, which is very important in the academy, where we want to walk mental circles around people in the theoretical realm. But in the UX world, it's much more connected to "What can you do?" I had to learn that the hard way at first by not getting jobs.

What did you bring from previous jobs and previous training? What do you think that gave you as a researcher?

It gave me an incredible toolbox, a backpack full of things to try. If one methodology doesn't work for a certain situation, it gave me the ability to know when to apply other types of methodologies and when to not. It's like when you're in an art class—you have to know the fundamentals before you can become a Picasso.

What are some of the stumbling blocks you see for people trying to break into UX research?

People don't think that their skills are transferable. If they have deeply researched the migratory patterns of the blue heron, they don't realize they can transfer their meticulous note-taking skills or gathering of data. They only see what they do apply to one type of thing. That's understanding your work in only one context. The stumbling block I see most often is people's inability to translate their skills into what are considered marketable skills. Not that they don't have them, they just don't know how to translate them.

Do you have any advice on how someone entering this field can get practical experience?

Get an account at a place like Upwork. Get people to pay you $20 to do a heuristic evaluation of their site. Starting out, it's an interesting side hustle where you can gain experience and also be compensated for your time. Go to conferences where you're able to continuously learn, and meet people doing the work and who have junior positions available or are willing to take a chance on a new person. You need to develop relationships with people who know how to build scaffolding for your career.

HOW TO GET EXPERIENCE

The goals of your resume and portfolio are to show off your skill set and your range as a researcher. But what should you do if you don't have a lot of experiences that translate to UX research? It feels intimidating, but there are lots of options that are great even for those who only have a little research-related experience. There are a few strategies that, regardless of your background, will really bolster your resume and portfolio. These include:

- Additional schooling or training
- Volunteer projects
- Internships

Let's dig a little deeper into each.

Additional schooling or training

Getting additional training is a really great way to jumpstart a career transition. What this looks like will vary from person to person and will depend on your situation. If you have the time, funds, and interest to get a graduate degree, do it! Grad school provides three things that benefit any career change: a certification that you have been trained in the skills needed for that new career, a place to practice those skills and create portfolio pieces, and a built-in network once you graduate.

Not everyone wants to or can go back to school for a career change, however. Instead, some folks use bootcamps or training programs to get the benefits of graduate school training without the time or cost of grad school. That being said, I don't recommend the full-time bootcamp intensives to people who aren't sure if they want to do research yet. Bootcamp intensives are several months long, require 40+ hours a week, and can be really pricey. The benefits of these bootcamps are the job-placement guarantees and the networking opportunities that are built into the programs.

Most UX bootcamps focus on UX design and only touch on research to the degree that a designer needs to know. For the cost and what you get out of it, it frequently doesn't make a lot of sense for people who want to move into UX research. If you want to be a designer who knows how to research, those programs are a great avenue and I know several successful designers who have gone that route.

Courses and workshops are useful for learning research fundamentals and for providing time and feedback to work on portfolio pieces. There are lots of UX certification classes and workshops out there that are worth the money. Here are some examples of certification resources to explore:

- Nielsen Norman Group courses

- University of Michigan UX research and design courses on Coursera

- Interaction Design Foundation

- Udemy UX courses

- General Assembly

    I'd recommend workshops or short classes instead of the bootcamp intensives, unless a designer role is your goal

- Continuing education courses at a community college.

- Certification programs from your local university

    A local to me example is the graduate level User-Centered Design (UCD) Certificate offered by the University of Washington in Seattle

- edX UX Experience Micromasters

- UX Micromasteries

These certificates might not be enough for some jobs at some companies. It's unlikely that you'll get your dream research job at Google or Amazon with only a few online learning courses under your belt. What you should get out of these courses and training, however, is a good grasp of the language that researchers use. You also have the space to practice research skills, opportunities for mentorship and feedback, and materials for a few good portfolio pieces. It won't score you your dream job out of the gate, but it will get you a foot in the door and the foundations you need to grow rapidly in a UX research career.

Volunteer projects

This next section comes with some caveats. Whether or not it's a good idea to volunteer for projects in order to get experience is hotly debated both in the general tech industry and in UX research. Your time is valuable and it's rarely appropriate to work for free. You might be a parent or a full-time professional and can't spare the time to do unpaid work. You might be a college student who could use that time to complete your degree, or you might work part-time and need those hours to make rent.

That being said, under some circumstances, volunteer projects can be a great way to add portfolio pieces and practice your skills. You should only consider it if:

- Volunteering your time will not be overly burdensome on your time or financial situation

- You want to break into a specific domain (e.g., foreign aid, healthcare) which requires specific knowledge and this project is a good opportunity to gain that experience and make connections

- You have a passion for their mission (e.g., working with homeless populations, non-profits, churches) and you know that organization wouldn't be able to afford paid UX services

- It doesn't take a lot of work to cultivate the opportunity

- You'll be given the room to grow your skills and make an impact

If one or more of those criteria apply, go for it! I've volunteered on small projects and for organizations whose missions resonate with me. Volunteer opportunities also give you exposure to a range of people, which is useful for researchers to cultivate empathy with a variety of life experiences.

When exploring a volunteer opportunity, consider asking if they would be able to pay you at least a small amount for your services. What that amount looks like really depends on your comfort level negotiating for a small fee and their ability to pay. Having that formality of fee for services offered is less about making any real money. There's an expectation of professionalism and responsibility that comes with charging for your work. It will make you feel more invested in the project (it's easy to de-prioritize work that isn't paying your bills), and it will make the organization a true client that expects a high-quality product from the money they spend on your services.

Internships

If you are switching careers later in life, the idea of an internship might be soul-crushing. It is humbling starting from the proverbial (and sometimes literal) bottom. For this reason, I don't often suggest internships as a career step for those switching careers. But if you are just out of college and eager to learn the industry, internships are a great way to break into UX research. As a bonus, nearly every research internship I have come across is paid, so you can afford to live while you learn. It's worth exploring what's available. Tech job fairs and UX job boards often post internship positions, and don't be shy about reaching out directly to researchers who work at a company you'd like to intern with. You'd be surprised, some of them may be interested and able to create an internship role for you!

Internships tend to pop up near universities that offer UX research or human-centered design degrees, so be prepared for these internships to be competitive or limited to recent college graduates. If you can score an internship, it goes a long way towards having a "UX research" line on your resume. During the internship, focus on making connections, demonstrating your skills, and setting up a new full-time opportunity, perhaps even at that same company.

BUILDING YOUR PORTFOLIO

Ok, now you have some experience. How do you demonstrate it? This is where a portfolio comes in handy. Before we dive into how to craft portfolio pieces, the jury is still out on whether UX researchers should be required to have a portfolio or not. Some researchers think portfolios aren't the right venue for translating or demonstrating research experience and projects, while others think they are critical pieces of your professional kit. In my opinion, it never hurts. Especially for your first UX research job, it can only help to show your experiences and provide the hiring committee with a fuller sense of who you are and how you work.

As I mentioned in Chapter 3, portfolio documents and/or links to a portfolio website are great to include in job applications or on your resume. SquareSpace, Weebly, or Wix are easy platforms to get started with a website. They have great looking templates and are low cost.

A researcher's portfolio will look very different from a designer's portfolio. A designer's portfolio showcases their artistic or innovative prototypes, print materials, or website layouts. A researcher's portfolio is a little squishier. Depending on the project you are highlighting in a portfolio piece, it could be a narrative or essay on a product's lifecycle or a brief research report on a usability study.

Now is the time to revisit the Experience List you made back in Chapter 2. What projects did you write down? What is the best way for you to describe the work you did, what your processes and results were, and what you did with those learnings? Try to pick out three to five different projects to highlight. You don't want to show only usability studies or include four survey projects. The goal of a portfolio is to show your range across various methods and approaches.

The best way to figure out what to include in a portfolio is to look at what others are doing! Check out these portfolios (also linked at iwantauxjob.com/chapter5) to get a sense of the spectrum:

- **My portfolio,** Senior Researcher, laurylzenobi.com

- **Elizabeth Kaufer,** Senior Researcher elizabethkaufer.com

- **Jason Lipshin,** Design Researcher jasonlipshin.net/ux-research-portfolio

- **Jules Lee,** Design Researcher
  juleslee.com

- **Emily Alter,** Senior Researcher
  emilyralter.com

- **Carl Pearson,** UX Researcher
  carljpearson.com

- **Jessica Bao,** UX Researcher
  jessicabao.me

Keep in mind, there's no perfect way to make a research portfolio. The most important things to include in each portfolio piece are:

- What was the problem/hypothesis?

- What methods did you use?

- What was your role? Was this an individual project, or did you work with a team? What were you responsible for?

- What choices did you make, and why? (For example, testing with certain groups of users, doing a rougher prototype early on the test versus using a more finished prototype, etc.)

- What constraints did you face? What did you do about those constraints? (Budgets, recruiting challenges, privacy or security concerns, etc.)

- What did you find out?

- What did you do with the results?

It's completely up to you how "designed" you want your portfolio to be. There are PDF or PowerPoint portfolios with lots of text and very little graphics, and there are complexly designed online portfolios with images of the entire prototype-to-product lifecycle. Choose what format will speak most to who you are as a researcher.

When deciding how to package your portfolio, think about where the best work-to-reward ratio is for you. If you want to learn how to code a site, then build your own portfolio website. If you want to have a more significant online presence, but don't want to code your own site, use a website generator like SquareSpace. The benefits of a portfolio website are they are much easier to share and list on a resume or job application, but they require more upfront work. If you prefer a portfolio with a lower lift, then stick with a PDF, PowerPoint, or even Google Drive doc that you can share as an attached document. This kind of portfolio is easy to tailor for each job and requires less upfront work relative to a website, which frees you up to work on other parts of your UX research transition.

Remember, this is a process. You don't need your resume and portfolio to be complete on day one. Instead, think of creating your resume and portfolio as opportunities to practice the craft of research and storytelling. Don't forget to get feedback from the community you've developed and the more-experienced UX researchers you've made friends with along the way.

This is an important part of gaining experience, so don't rush it! You'll want your portfolio and resume to look good for Chapter 7!

WHAT TO READ NOW

iwantauxjob.com/chapter5

Mitchell Wakefield, "UX Research Career Starter Guide"

Yuling An, "How to Break into the Field of UX Research"

Nielson Norman Group, "Portfolios for UX Researchers: Top 10 Recommendations"

Nikki Anderson, "Storytelling for a UX Research Portfolio"

DONNA'S UX STORY

Donna Andrews

Donna has been a UX researcher for over 18 years and is a UX Research Manager at a real estate company. She's seen the field of UX grow and change remarkably over her nearly two decades of experience as a researcher. We talked at length about the trends she's seen and what she thinks that means for the field as a whole for new researchers.

Tell me about how you got started as a researcher. What has been your career path?

I was in a linguistics PhD program and realized I needed something different. I answered a resume call from Microsoft for linguistic testers. It turned out they weren't hiring researchers right then, but they did need a "usability engineer" for the natural language search product. I read Usability Engineering by Jakob Nielsen to prepare for the interview. I was completely unqualified and had no idea what I was doing for at least six months, although the impostor syndrome lasted for years.

You have a fascinating background, researchers from a linguistics background aren't common.

It's probably because it happened long enough ago, the HCI [Human-Computer Interaction] field was not established as it is now. I joined Microsoft in 2001. At the time, there were people from all different areas. One person had a kinesiology background. Another person came from library sciences. It was a reasonably small team—the group manager had an ergonomics background.

We just don't have that anymore. Everybody does a HCI masters or a certificate. I honestly think it's sad in a way, because we lose the diversity that we had at the time.

I'm working with a woman right now who has a PhD in Biomedical Informatics. She is invaluable because of the perspective that she brings. No one on the team can do this stuff that she's doing. She's junior in terms of being a UX researcher, but she's literally the only person that can do half of what we need done.

How has research changed since you started?

It wasn't a discipline. It was a couple of books. It was you read Don Norman's The Design of Everyday Things, and you read Jakob Nielsen's Usability Engineering. Literally, I read Jakob Nielsen's book in order to go to my interview. To this day, I don't know how I got through that interview. I had super-supportive managers in my first job. I had so much support. That was key.

I'm happy that it's become a discipline. I think it's great.

How have you found jobs?

What I've done since Microsoft is I've followed people that I like to work with. I asked people who I enjoyed working with where they were going next, and I would follow them. I like to work with people that I trust. Networking groups like Hexagon (a Seattle-based UX community) are great for support and connections.

Just sending in your resume doesn't work. You need to have someone who looks at your resume and understands it. Build and nurture a network of people who know you. Then use that network to find jobs.

Any ideas on how to make yourself stand out as a new researcher?

People don't tell enough stories! The interviews I remember are ones where the candidate told us a great story. We had an interviewee once tell us about an animated kids recipe book project he worked on. Another interviewee told us about this passion project he did for his diabetic son to monitor his sugar levels. That kind of storytelling makes people feel a lot more human and helps them stand out.

If you need stories to tell, come up with silly or weird research questions, like, "What are people's perceptions of whales?" Do guerrilla research at Starbucks where you interview people and give them a Starbucks gift card. Pick a random topic you want to learn about, do the research, and then call it a project and put it on your resume. Use the methods and tools of UX research that you have available to you, and practice your craft that way. Then, in interviews, tell your stories.

HOW TO FIND JOBS

Half the struggle of any job search is knowing where to actually look for jobs. Since UX research is still a growing industry, there are creative ways to find a UX role in addition to more traditional ones. These include:

- Networking
- Job boards
- Internships
- Finding or creating a UX role at your current job

Networking to find jobs works well for many people but can be a horrible experience for others. The key thing to know about networking is it doesn't have to feel slimy. Go to events, reach out to your UX community that you're building, and use that time to simply connect with people. The goal of networking is to make friends and build social capital, with the thought that eventually those connections might benefit all parties professionally. Think of networking as a long game—it may not pay off immediately, but as you grow your career and your skills, the relationships you foster in your UX community can lead to job referrals in the future.

UX-focused job boards are where you should focus your job search time. Large aggregator boards like Indeed or Monster tend to post generic roles that hundreds of people will apply to, so you as a new researcher are likely to get lost in the sea of applications. LinkedIn is the exception to the rule when it comes to large aggregator sites because those that are hiring will often post in specific groups like the User Experience Design group I mentioned in Chapter 3. In sum, the less anonymous and generic the posting platform, the higher quality the job and the likelier you are to get a person to read your resume.

Focus on jobs that are posted to UX job boards like the Mixed Methods #jobs channel or UX Jobs. Here are some job boards to check out (linked at iwantauxjob.com/chapter6):

- Mixed Methods slack group #jobs channel
- UXPA Job Bank
- UX Jobs Board
- Tech Ladies Jobs Board
- Just UX Jobs
- We Work Remotely Jobs
- IxDA Jobs
- EPIC Jobs Board

- Remotive Remote Jobs Board
- LinkedIn and Facebook groups listed in Chapter 3

When looking for jobs, remember that there are multiple paths to a researcher role, so don't limit yourself to "UX researcher" postings. Associate researchers, UX writers, UX coordinators, or UX analysts are all excellent entry points to a researcher role and might be less competitive than researcher listings.

Internships are often used as an extended interview for permanent positions, and it's not uncommon for interns to be offered a job at the end of their internship period. Internships are great opportunities to get your foot in the door. Especially early in your career transition, the more face-to-face time you have with potential employers, the better your chances of getting hired. Employers are more likely to take a risk on a new researcher that they know versus one that they don't.

Lastly, you might be able to create a UX position at your current company or volunteer organization by moving to a research position internally or even adjusting your current job to take on more research responsibilities. You might not be able to take on a full researcher role in your current job or company, but if you're able to take on a new title that's more closely related to research (or take on other UX or research duties), that can go a long way towards making your resume match where you are on your research transition.

This was the strategy I took with my first job out of graduate school. As I mentioned in earlier chapters, I was working at a non-profit where I managed a print production. My original job description did not have any research or UX duties, but over the course of my first year in the job, I started to do customer research and investigate ways to improve the product that I managed.

What began as customer phone interviews extended into surveys and additional interviews, and by the end of my first year, I produced a research brief that outlined ways to improve the customer experience of both the print product and its associated website. During this time, I successfully lobbied for a title change and the ability to add more research activities to my daily work. I leveraged my existing job to practice research skills and create portfolio pieces. At the end of my two years with the company, the research I conducted was used to restructure the product and enact large changes to the website.

Are there ways to carve out a research position in your current job or company? Most likely, yes. See if you could make a lateral move by looking for internal research positions or positions that would benefit from doing research. If you work in sales and want to do more research, could you transition to a marketing team that does customer insights research? If you know your company has UX research roles, could you petition the UX manager to create an internship or associate research role for you? Consider that when you make a UX role for yourself at your current company, it doesn't have to be a "UX research" title per se. If the new role gives you room to practice research skills, it could be a useful transition to a UX research role in the future.

WHAT TO READ NOW

iwantauxjob.com/chapter6

Ellen Twomey, "How to Get an Entry Level UX Job in 3 Months"

Oz, "How to Get a UX Job with No Professional UX Experience"

The Ladders, "6 smart tips for turning your internship into a full-time job"

JIMMY'S UX STORY

Jimmy McConnell is a UX researcher at a government contracting firm where he helps government agencies build better solutions for medical settings. Jimmy speaks to the importance of leveraging your interests and past experience and the value of professional skills in your future UX career.

How did you know you wanted to do user research?

I just kind of stumbled into it. I have done research my whole life, mostly science/medical-type research, but I wanted something a little more fast-paced and meaningful. I always found tech interesting and knew that UX was a growing field and knew that a university near me (University of Baltimore) offered masters courses focused on UX research.

Tell me about how you got started as a researcher!

I started off doing psychological and bio-medical research in undergrad because I thought I wanted to become a doctor and those seemed like good options to increase my skills and resume experiences. Most of my undergrad research was focused on social psychology, neuroscience, and fMRI research. After undergrad, I decided to do more community psychology research (focused on substance use) because I wanted to make sure my research had a positive impact on my community. I was looking for something a little more person-facing compared to the data-heavy quantitative research that I had gotten used to in undergrad. I worked for a private substance use research firm in Baltimore as a research assistant for three years before deciding to pursue more education for a career in UX research.

What do you think your previous jobs/educational experiences gave you as a researcher?

I think that my previous research experience gave me a great foundation for good research practices, analysis, and best institutional practices. I learned how best to perform in a professional setting, how to keep up with data/paperwork management, working with tools like Excel and other analysis platforms, as well as building up my interpersonal skills from having to work with hundreds of participants.

How would you talk about the job market for user research?

I would say that the UX research market is hard to get into but easy to stay in, given that you are good at your job and actually take an interest in the work. The market itself is hungry for experienced researchers, but most postings don't appear to want fresh, green researchers in favor of established ones. This can make it hard to get a job. But now that I'm in the field, I am constantly being messaged or recruited on LinkedIn for job postings.

How did you find research jobs?

To be honest, I have received all of my UX research jobs by word-of-mouth from friends that already work in the field, or by contracting with other companies to perform UX research.

What do you wish you could tell past-you when you first got started as a researcher?

Be patient and work at the speed of your team. Don't try to excel at everything all at once. Research itself sounds easy, but there is a finesse to research practices that takes time to acquire and perfect. Just keep introducing yourself to new methodologies and research practices, and eventually choosing your own plan will become second nature.

What do you think makes a good researcher?

Patience, the ability to have an unbiased/solution-focused opinion, the ability to get along with just about anybody, intellectual curiosity, the ability to see each tree and the forest (in terms of data and issues), and more patience.

How do you think the field of user research has changed since you started practicing?

I think that the field has matured in a sense that it is becoming ubiquitous amongst software development firms. I think that the "oh, we should actually speak to our users when building a product" attitude has become more openly accepted as a part of the development process.

INTERVIEWING

This is where the rubber hits the road. Interviews are where you'll demonstrate everything you've learned. Interviews can also be terrifying and stress-inducing, especially if you aren't sure how to best prepare for them. Knowing how to prepare and what to prepare for is the most effective way to reduce that stress and present your best self in an interview. So, in this chapter, we'll break down the interview process into three phases:

- Before the interview
- During the interview
- After the interview

In each phase we'll go over what to expect in each phase and how to prepare.

BEFORE THE INTERVIEW

To best prepare for an interview, you need to know what the hiring committee's goals are. Thankfully, there are some basics that every hiring committee will look for during an interview.

- What are the candidate's experience and expertise in various research methods? (i.e., how well developed are their "hard skills"?)

- What are the candidate's personality and work style like? (i.e., how are their "soft skills"?)

- Do #1 and #2 align with the job requirements and company culture?

Different companies have different strategies on how to evaluate these three characteristics. If you want to work at a big company like Amazon or Google, there's plenty written about how to master these interviews. These companies have very rigorous interview processes, so reading these guides can be a useful way to prepare for an interview at any company.

All companies will want to get a sense of your research skill level. They might assess your skill level through a *mock research session*, where an interviewer poses as a user and you demonstrate how you would conduct a research session with that user. The hiring committee might also ask you to create a research plan before the interview, and then spend time during the interview talking over what you created. It's more common with design interviews, but the interviewers may ask you to prepare a brief talk about one of your portfolio pieces.

To prepare for a mock research session, practice running a usability or open-ended conversation with a friend or family member. Get their feedback on how comfortable you seemed and whether or not you asked open-ended questions. Have them warn you if you asked any leading questions. Do a few run-throughs until you feel confident in your moderation style.

If you are asked to prepare a *research plan*, use the prompt the interviewers provide to select the appropriate method or research questions. Make a list of all the research methodologies you know or have used and walk through when you would or wouldn't use each one. The method you choose will depend on the questions that you need answered, and the number of users you need to talk to will depend on the method you choose. Remember, research goals inform the method, which in turn will inform who and how many users you talk to. Keep the research plan to one or two pages. The interviewers want to see how you justify research decisions, so practice succinctly explaining your choices.

A *portfolio talk* is when you'll give a short presentation on a past research project as part of the interview. Use the presentation to explain your research approach and process. The recruiter or hiring committee will let you know how long the presentation should be and how many projects they want you to present. The interviewers want to see how you handle public speaking, so practice your talk to the point where you feel prepared but not scripted.

When you prepare, outline what you want to say with bullet points or post-it notes rather than writing it out word-for-word. As you practice, that will help you avoid trying to "memorize the script" and make it feel more natural.

You'll be asked questions about your research choices and results after you present, so think through what they could ask about each portfolio piece. Some example questions they might ask you are:

- Why did you choose to run a survey instead of doing user interviews?

- How do you know you talked to enough users?

- What did you do with the results?

- What would you do differently?

The hiring team or recruiter will give you a sense of what to expect for each of these interview exercises—e.g., for a portfolio talk, they want you to present two projects and take no more than thirty minutes. If you don't receive any guidance from the hiring team, that's a good time to show you are comfortable taking the initiative to clarify situations and ask them what to expect.

In addition to these interview exercises, you'll have at least one traditional interview conversation with the hiring team. Let's go over some general interviewing strategies so that you are comfortable with the format.

How to approach interviews

It took me a few years to realize that interviews are just glorified conversations, and you can make conversation with anybody for an hour. That helped me relax about the process of interviewing, which can be really terrifying. They can feel like you are auditioning for a paycheck. I usually feel incredibly vulnerable during this phase of the job search. Interviews will always be stressful, but if you can change your outlook and loosen your expectations, it will flow more easily.

Some of the best advice I've ever received about getting into the flow of public speaking also applies to interviews. Professional speakers get just as nervous as novice speakers, but they embrace that nervousness instead of trying to tamp it down. In Confessions of a Public Speaker (2011), Scott Berkun tells us that the reason public speaking is so nerve-wracking is because our brains respond to speaking in front of others in the same way it would respond when faced with a lion alone in a field. No matter how many talks a professional speaker has given, they still get nervous. I get sweaty and jittery before a speaking event or an interview, but because I know that's ok and normal, I can channel that energy from unproductive anxiety into productive excitement by spending more time researching the company, going for a jog the day of the interview, or doing practice runs of my portfolio samples the day before. Preparation is one of the best ways to calm down your brain's public-speaking fear response. As Scott says, "My intent is to simply know my material so well that I'm comfortable with it. Confidence, not perfection, is the goal." Aim to approach interviews in the same way. Be confident and comfortable in your material - your resume, experiences, and what you bring to the role.

Try to approach the interview and job application process as a fun experiment. Change up your stories and resume each time and see what works best—it's an A/B test in its own right! Immediately after each interview, spend thirty minutes taking notes. What stories seemed to resonate better than others? What stories did you struggle to tell? Were there any metrics you couldn't remember at the time that you should brush up on? Remember, even if it feels like it, there is no shortage of UX jobs in the world. You have the time and space to experiment.

Get comfortable telling your story. Interviews, especially for researchers, are all about story-telling. Pull from your portfolio materials. Tell the story of your path to UX research and speak to how your past experiences translate to UX research. Explicitly call out examples of hard and soft skills. For example:

> In my previous experience as a clinical counselor, I ran a long-term survey that looked at changes in mood based on patient exposure to art therapy and physical activity. This generated a large dataset, which a colleague and I managed and analyzed. The results were really impressive! For the patient group that had

both art therapy and regular exercise classes, there
was a 10% reduction in patient-reported severity of
clinical depression. Using these results, I advocated for
a change in our curriculum with our board of directors.
I'm excited to translate my data analytic skills and my
experience convincing my clinic leadership into a UX
research role, as I see a lot of application of those skills
in the work that this company does.

What about that example works? If I heard that from a candidate in
a hiring process, I would immediately know they can concisely bring
me along with a logical narrative that outlines the problem statement
(clinical study looking at art and activity exposure), the methodology
(survey and a sense of scale of data with a large dataset), collaboration
(worked with a colleague), and a demonstrated research impact (10%
reduction, convinced directors to implement changes). Sure, that candidate might not have UX research experience specifically, but they
have shown me that they have both the hard and soft skills. If that mix
of skills is what my company is looking for, that candidate is a good fit.

Look through your experiences and pull out a few choice stories that
you feel demonstrate both the depth and range of your hard and soft
skills. Once you have those experiences selected, write up a quick two-
to-three-minute narrative.

The STAR method, which stands for Situation—Task—Action—
Result, is a good format for structuring narratives, especially if the
interviewer asks you questions that prompt you to tell them a story.

Situation
Describe the scenario and set the stage.

Task
What was your role in the situation?

Action

What actions did you take?

Result

What was the outcome of your actions?

Run your two-to-three-minute narratives by your friends and loved ones as practice. Ask people in your UX community, such as a past informational interviewee or informal mentor, if they would listen to your narratives and give you feedback. Practice your stories until you know them backward and forward. The advice for portfolio-piece preparation applies here as well. Write out S, T, A, and R on four post-it notes, one letter on each. Jot down a few keywords on each post-it note. Practice telling the story from start to end using the post-it notes as triggers for each section of the story.

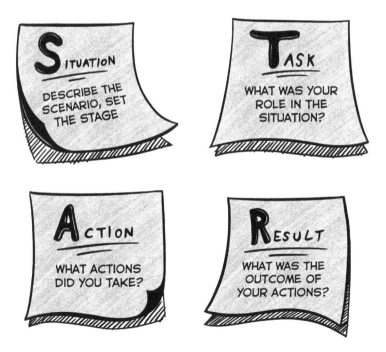

HOW THE STAR METHOD
WORKS IN ACTION

Question

Tell me about a time you helped a coworker figure out the best method to answer a research question?

Things to touch on in your response

What is this question trying to learn about you? The hiring team wants to know: How do you approach new research requests? What sort of clarification questions do you ask to get to the root of the problem? How do you take initiative?

Response

At my last job, my project manager approached me with a research question. They wanted to know why users were abandoning items in their online shopping cart, and they thought a survey might be the right way to figure that out. As the only one on the team with experience running surveys, I was unsure that a survey was the best method to use without knowing more about the project goals. So I took initiative to ask my project manager more questions about what they wanted to learn from this research and what sort of constraints they had with budget or timing. I learned that we had about a month to work on this research question, and my project manager was interested in learning about how people used the shopping cart. So I suggested that our first step should be to bring in a few users for a quick lab session where we could watch how they purchase items. From that research, I realized that users thought of our shopping cart as a way to save items that they wanted to purchase in the future, and so abandoning the cart wasn't necessarily a bad thing. I suggested that we also implement a "wish list" feature so that users could create a short list of future purchases that they could save outside of their cart.

That response shows a solid understanding of when and why to use certain research methodologies. It drives home your collaborative approach towards uncovering the root cause of an issue instead of taking a research request at face value. At the same time, you are gently moving the project manager away from "leading with method" (i.e., prescribing how they want you to answer the question) and asking them to help you formulate the high-level research goals of this work. Asking about their team's needs and deadlines shows that you are thinking about how to scope the project so it can be successful.

Here's another example of a question that you can answer with a story:

Question

What got you interested in research and why are you interested in this role?

Things to touch on in your response

Talk about your path to research! This is where your practice with framing your experiences can truly shine. Do research on this company or role before your interview. What excites you about this opportunity? This is where you can flatter the hiring committee a bit.

Response

I've always been interested in people and why they do things. That's why I got my graduate degree in sociology. Throughout my career, I've incorporated human-centered approaches, which has been my favorite part about my previous jobs. I'm excited to transition full-time to research, especially at a company like yours where I can make a big impact on how people find healthcare services. Your company is leading the charge in identifying barriers to medical access, which I find a challenging and rewarding field. My previous experiences in the healthcare industry will be a great asset to my work as a researcher at this company because I'm familiar with the lingo in the field and have experience working with patients.

If you want more practice answering interview prompts, here's a sample list of questions to start with:

- How do you convince stakeholders on the value of usability research?

- When do you know you've tested with enough users?

- Describe a research or design decision you made that wasn't popular. How did you handle it?

- How do you know if you are asking the right research questions for a project?

- Tell me about a time when you worked on multiple projects. How did you prioritize?

- What has been your most challenging research project? What was challenging about it? How did you overcome those challenges?

- Pick a favorite app. How would you design a research study to evaluate it?

- Someone on the team has a strong opinion about how a certain feature should be designed, but you disagree about whether it would be a good user experience. How do you approach the situation?

- Why do you want to work at this company?

- How would you improve on our company's product?

Now that we've touched on what to expect from an interview cycle and how to prepare for different types of interviews, let's talk about what to do during the interview.

DURING THE INTERVIEW

It's easy to get so caught up in hoping the interviewers like us that we forget interviews are also opportunities for you to decide if that job is a good fit for you. As much as the hiring team is evaluating you, you should be considering if this is the role that will fit the culture you want to work in and where you want to grow in your career. Let's say that working as a solo researcher is not what you want in your first UX role. How do you bring that up in an interview? It doesn't feel quite right to come out and say, "I don't want to work alone because I'm new at this." Here's another way to frame that question: "I'm early in my UX career, and finding a role where there's support and mentorship on the team is important to me. What does the team structure for this role look like?"

Explore what is important to you in your first UX role. Is it a mission you feel passionate about? The work culture, the ability to work remotely, childcare on-site, opportunities for career growth? Is it just straight up the salary?

Come up with two or three make-or-break qualities in a job that excite you. Pull your Experience List out and look at your Why UX column. Are there items or qualities listed that are really important to you? Create questions to ask your interviewers that uncover if that job has those qualities. The answers they provide will help you decide if a particular role is a good fit for you and a place where you can succeed.

The last ten or fifteen minutes of an interview are usually set aside for you to ask questions of the hiring team. This is a great time to learn more about the job, the team, the organization and its culture, and see if it matches your two or three make-or-break qualities. It's also an opportunity for you to differentiate yourself as a candidate and prove your skills as a researcher who asks good questions. Research the company before the interview and have a few insightful questions to ask in your back pocket. Take notes during the interview with any follow-up questions and use this time at the end of the interview to dive deeper.

If you find out early in the hiring process that the position is not going to be a good fit, let them know. You can always walk away from the hiring process!

Here are some ideas for make-or-break qualities and questions to ask:

Make or Break		
WHY UX	MAKE-OR-BREAK QUALITIES	QUESTIONS TO ASK DURING THE INTERVIEW
- COLLABORATION - CAREER OPPORTUNITIES - IMPROVE USERS' LIVES	- WORKING ON A TEAM IS IMPORTANT TO ME - OPPORTUNITIES TO ADVANCE MY CAREER AND HAVE SUPPORT - HAVING AN IMPACT ON PRODUCT DEVELOPMENT	- WHAT IS THE TEAM STRUCTURE LIKE AT THIS COMPANY/DEPARTMENT? - WHAT PROFESSIONAL DEVELOPMENT OPPORTUNITIES DOES THIS ROLE HAVE? - ARE THERE MENTORSHIP OPPORTUNITIES? - HOW HAS RESEARCH IMPACTED YOUR PRODUCT DEVELOPMENT IN THE PAST?

AFTER THE INTERVIEW

Once you get past the interviews and have a job offer in hand, it's time to negotiate! Unless you're accepting an internship or similar type of position where the stipend or salary is truly fixed, you should always negotiate your compensation. There are lots of different levers to work with here. Common things to negotiate for are more vacation time, higher salary, starting bonus, moving/relocation bonuses (if relevant), subsidies that are important to you (e.g., health insurance, childcare, bus stipend). Very few things are off the table, and the worst thing that the company can say is no.

It can be intimidating to negotiate, especially if you are worried that you've gotten this far in the process and you don't want to ruin your chances of getting hired by negotiating. At this point, the company has decided they want to work with you, and they've spent a great deal of time and resources on interviews and recruiting to get you to this point. It doesn't make a lot of sense for them to lose you as a candidate because you asked to negotiate. It's actually expected! If a company does decide to rescind their offer to you because you asked to negotiate compensation, you did not want to work for them, as much as that might hurt in the moment. Any company willing to drop you at that stage would likely not be a great place to work.

I won't attempt to recreate the wheel on negotiation strategies, as there are a lot of resources already out there. But know this: the best leverage you have during a negotiation is a competing offer, so try to interview at multiple places at the same time.

Check out these resources (not exhaustive):

- Women for Hire
- Josh Doody's Salary Negotiation Tactics
- Alison Doyle's Proven Tactics for Negotiating a Higher Salary
- Patrick McKenzie's Salary Negotiation: Make More Money, Be More Valued

Remember, interviewing can be fun and it's only one step in the process! An interview is just one part of becoming a UX researcher. All the other steps we've talked about in this book—crafting a resume, building a portfolio, gaining experience—are the hard parts. The interview is your chance to demonstrate all the hard work you've already put into this process.

──── WHAT TO READ OR WATCH NOW ────

iwantauxjob.com/chapter7

Douglas Pyle, "I interviewed 217 UX candidates for open roles last year; here's what works and what doesn't"

Eleonora Zucconi, "46 Interview Questions for User Experience Researchers at Google, Amazon, Microsoft and Facebook"

Melissa Hui, "Cracking The UX Researcher Interview"

Oz, "The 4 Types of UX Interview Questions to Master"

Sarah Doody, "How to prepare for a UX job interview?"

CareerFoundry, "5 Questions You'll Be Asked In Your UX Research Job Interview"

Kevin Liang, "UX Researcher Job Interview TIPS | How to Prepare for UX Recruiter Call & Hiring Manager PART 1"

Kevin Liang, "UX Researcher ONSITE Job Interview | Portfolio & 1 on 1 Interviews | PART 2 | Zero to UX"

Indeed, "How to Use the STAR Interview Response Technique"

WHAT NOW?

Congratulations! You've made it through the book. Along the way, you've learned everything you need to know about the seven steps of becoming a UX researcher. You have an understanding of what it takes to reframe yourself and your skills, you've started to craft your portfolio, you're networking like wild, and you're putting your resume out there.

WHERE DO YOU
GO FROM HERE?

Welcome to Step 8. Step 8 is where you keep learning. Step 8 is where you build on everything that you've laid out in Steps 1 through 7. Step 8 is where you start to talk about yourself as a UX researcher. Step 8 is where the journey really takes off.

Your path will have ups and down, progress and setbacks. It will be a little fuzzy sometimes. If you're ever unsure of your next steps, come back to this book. Lean on the communities you found during this process. Go to a research meetup. When in doubt, keep learning.

The process of becoming a researcher is very much like the process of research itself. Things start out fuzzy but move towards clarity. Career transition author Herminia Ibarra says, "We like to think that we can leap directly from a desire for change to a single decision that will complete our 'reinvention.' As a result, we remain naïve about the long, essential testing period where our actions transform fuzzy, undefined possibilities into concrete choices we can evaluate." Think about this time where you start to transform into a UX researcher as your testing period.

It took me over a year of skill-building and six months of job searching to land my first UX role. I look back on those long months as a formative period that gives me deep empathy for those in a similar position as I was a few years ago—unhappy with a career path, interested in learning a new field, and unsure of what to do next. The months I spent formulating myself into a UX researcher were emotionally charged. I experienced guilt at wanting to "leave behind" my academic training and community for a "sell-out" job in the private sector. I had a crisis of identity—could I still call myself an anthropologist if I decided not to continue my graduate work and instead go into the workforce? More fundamentally, was I outgoing enough to be able to talk to strangers as a researcher? Was I confident enough to show up to a researcher interview having no research roles on my resume? I was often a hot mess. To get by, I channeled that energy into productive exercises like building portfolio pieces, reading every single book I could get my hands on, and learning how to code and build a website.

The most common concerns I hear from my mentees who want to become researchers is their lack of confidence and their insecurity that they have the experience to actually make the jump. I wrote this book to give you the confidence and the framework you need to make that brave leap into the uncomfortable space of transition. It takes effort, but that effort is what helps you grow your confidence as a researcher.

I know this will work for you, and when it does, I want to hear from you! It's just about my favorite thing to hear back from people two, six, or twelve months later when they've landed their first UX research role.

Please send me an email at

lauryl@iwantauxjob.com

and let me know how your
UX research transition went.

STAY CURIOUS!

CPSIA information can be obtained
at www.ICGtesting.com
Printed in the USA
BVHW091833140621
609554BV00014B/616